SHIP DIORAMAS

BRINGING YOUR MODELS TO LIFE

SHIP DIORAMAS
BRINGING YOUR MODELS TO LIFE

DAVID GRIFFITH

Seaforth
PUBLISHING

Copyright © David Griffith 2013

First published in Great Britain in 2013 by
Seaforth Publishing
An imprint of Pen & Sword Books Ltd
47 Church Street, Barnsley
S Yorkshire S70 2AS

www.seaforthpublishing.com
Email info@seaforthpublishing.com

British Library Cataloguing in Publication Data
A CIP data record for this book is available from the British Library

ISBN 978-1-84832-168-7

Typeset and designed by Neil Sayer
Printed in China through Printworks Int. Ltd.

CONTENTS

INTRODUCTION

This book had its origins in my previous book, *Ship Models from Kits – Basic and Advanced Techniques for Small Scales* published in 2009. At the time it came out I thought that I did not have another book in me, and that I was more of a J D Salinger, rather than a Clive Cussler. But the publishers, Seaforth, were pleased with the book and I wondered if there might be another lurking somewhere. This little volume is the result.

I am taking as my subject, the art of the ship diorama. These form a specific sub-genre within ship modelling in general, and many people may be somewhat intimidated by the idea. I know that I am not the greatest diorama-maker in history, but I think I understand what makes a good one, and why others are not so good. I hope that I can take some of the mystique out of the subject, and encourage you to give it a go if you have not already done so.

So, let me now say what this book is not about. It is not primarily about how to make model ships. If you are looking for a good 'how to' book on this subject, do not buy this one. I would suggest instead that you get my previous book, which will give you precisely what you want. You may well have bought it already. In that case I will say to you, 'Thank you very much, and treat yourself to this one as well, anyway!' If you have not already bought it, then go on, be a devil, buy both of them! After all, it's no more than 364 days till your next birthday, and it may even be Christmas before then, too!

There is perhaps rather more emphasis in this book on ideas and inspiration. I am talking rather more about 'what' you are trying to do, 'why' you might do it in a particular way, and maybe even 'whether' it is appropriate to do it at all. Nevertheless, you will still find plenty of places where I tell you 'how' to go about it.

My previous book received a bit of justified criticism for the rather confusing layout of the text and pictures. I take full responsibility for this, and believe that it was due to my inexperience in writing and lack of knowledge of the publishing process. It was certainly not the fault of the publishers or their layout artist, who took at least three attempts to make something printable from the text and photos that I sent in.

Some readers were also a bit disappointed that I dealt almost exclusively with 1/700 scale models. I make no apology for this, as it is the scale in which I am most at home working. In Europe 1/700 is a more popular scale than 1/350 or larger, which are more favoured in the USA. I'm afraid that this book will be even more slanted towards 1/700, as the smaller scale is much more practical for dioramas, and there are currently far more accessories in this scale available on the market. Large scale dioramas have the potential for taking up an enormous amount of storage space and are difficult to display.

As well as dioramas that I have made, and which I shall take you through the process of planning and building, I am also going to showcase the work of other modellers that

I admire. Sometimes this will be because they are excellent or inspiring examples of the art; others will illustrate a particular point that I wish to make. The work of some of these people is far better than anything I can do myself. I should like to thank all of them for sending me photographs, and letting me share them with you. The modellers that I feature, starting at the west and working east, are: Mike McCabe, Jim Baumann, Don McKeand, Peter Fulgoney, Bruno Gire, Jean Mahieux, Werner De Keersmaecker, the model makers on the island of Texel, Guido Hopp, Christian Bruer, Torben Keitel, Frank Spahr, György Pék and Katarzyna Manikowska.

I should also like to express my gratitude to Ellen, my wife, who has been patient and encouraging in equal measure, and put up with being ignored for many weekends and evenings.

This book has been a long time in its gestation. That is because I built eight dioramas specifically for the book. Compare that with the two ships that I built for the previous one, and take into account being side-tracked by wanting to paint some metal figures at times, and it is not surprising that it has taken so long. My wife did not think it would ever happen.

But it has.

David Griffith
Glasgow, March 2013

CHAPTER I

MODELS IN CONTEXT

As I said in the Introduction, this book is not about how to build kits of model ships. This book is much more about taking those model ships, and putting them into context. By this I mean such ideas as: setting them in a realistic environment, be that sea, harbour or dockside, showing the relationships between different ships or boats, illustrating the various activities that may happen on or around ships, telling a story or suggesting an emotion.

I'm sure all model makers put their work into a form of context all the time. If you think about it, every time a child picks up a toy aeroplane and runs with it, making buzzing noises, he is putting it into context. It is the same thing when he pushes a little tank along the carpet, saying, 'Pow, pow, pow!' and flicking the Airfix soldiers over. We do the same thing as adults. Admit it, how many times have you picked up a model ship and held it in front of your face, moving it in a sort of corkscrew fashion, as though it is pushing through a heavy ocean swell? I do it all the time, and you do too, don't you? That feels better already, doesn't it? Recognising your inner child. End of psychology lesson!

Before I go any further, I should like to try and explain what I am meaning in this book when I talk about dioramas, because I am thinking in rather broader and less distinct terms than the people who define competition classes. These need precise and careful definitions so that similar models are judged against one another. The rules may include such matters as: comprising more that one model, being on other than a plain base, inclusion of figures that are not on the model itself, telling a story or illustrating a theme. I really could not care less about these rulebook classifications.

For me it is all about doing something with, or to, a model to improve the sense of reality. Some of the models that I shall show you, if entered in a diorama class, might find themselves moved because a judge said, 'That's not a diorama, it's only a single ship'. And, do you know what? I really couldn't be bothered, one way or t'other; I build models to satisfy myself, not the judges. It is

the achievement of an apparent reality that is important to me.

On the other hand, I used to have good natured arguments with a friend of mine who ran the competitions at the Scottish IPMS Nationals. I would place my models in the category for single ships, only to find them moved into that for ship dioramas. When pressed, Geoff would say, 'It's got crew figures on it. That makes it a diorama.'

I would then point out that using the same logic, every tank that had its commander's head poking out of the turret ought also to be regarded as a diorama. As they say, the judge's decision is final, and my models would usually stay in the diorama class, which would be smaller than the one for single ships, and the competition proportionately less intense. After all, winning a silver medal in a class of two means precisely nothing. The boxer who is knocked out by the first punch still comes second.

I am speaking of this simply in order to illustrate the arbitrary nature of the definitions that are used to decide what a diorama is. In the course of this book, I shall be using the term very loosely. Please do not get hot under the collar about it. What I am going to try to show you is not how to win a competition, but how to have an artistic approach to your modelling, and impart an air of reality to your work.

So, what sort of things ought we to be building? What should our creations consist of?

I built dioramas as a child, during my AFV period. Like many of us, I am now embarrassed when I recall them, not so much because of the lack of modelling skills, but mainly because it was obvious that I had no idea of what I was conveying or how I was arranging the various components. I particularly remember one that had a base about eighteen inches square. A ditch went straight across with a knocked out 1/72 Airfix assault gun nose down in it. There was also a makeshift bridge from unpainted balsa wood, and a few Airfix figures running around, but precious little else. It was, I suppose, trying to tell a story of sorts, but it broke every rule of composition or proportion.

I mention this childhood effort because it illustrates the point that it is not enough simply to have a variety of components in a diorama; it requires that thought and imagination are employed to use them appropriately, melding them into a cohesive and satisfying whole.

Although the description 'diorama' is a useful shorthand word, and I continue to use it, I prefer to think in terms of models in a realistic context, and what they are trying to show or tell. I would suggest that there are a number of features, which, if incorporated into a model, will transform it into a diorama. There is no need to have all of them, just one of them might suffice, but having two or three would result in a much stronger composition. But trying to put all of them into a single model will risk producing something that is too busy and loses any focus on its central theme.

Such features include (but there will be others):
- More than one ship, or extra smaller vessels
- Shoreline or dockside
- Depiction of a relationship between vessels
- Human activity
- Industrial, military or naval activity
- Combat (but with major reservations regarding naval subjects)
- Depiction of a dramatic incident, either historical or imaginary
- Reproduction of some famous photograph or painting
- Depiction of an emotion

Similar features would apply to the dioramas produced by our colleagues in the armour modelling fraternity, and they have certain advantages over us ship modellers. Vehicles can pass very close to each other and can therefore be shown together on a base of reasonable size. Land combat can take place at close quarters and is therefore a suitable subject for a diorama for the same reason. If the human body is represented at a scale of 1/35, or even 1/76, it is possible to show posture, gesture and even facial expression. Such subtleties are denied to ship modellers working in small scales, and we have to express ourselves with metaphorical broad strokes. That, and we have to regard the ships as the personalities in our creations.

In addition, I think that there are certain basic characteristics that good dioramas ought to show, and I should like to discuss these, before moving on to give examples of ideas for good dioramas, and bad ideas that are best avoided.

A diorama should be visually pleasing and mentally satisfying

This is a very vague statement, and almost impossible to define. It is easier to give examples of what would make it unpleasing or unsatisfying. If you look at a painting that you think is perfect, it is very hard to say why that is so. In a painting that you thoroughly dislike, the bad points are usually pretty obvious.

The construction and finishing should be as good as we are capable of. We all have different skill levels, and that is quite OK, just as long as we are trying to do the best we can. But don't look at work that is substandard for you and say, 'That's alright, I'll just put it into a diorama and no one will notice.' It will still be seen, perhaps even more so, as the eye is drawn in, to give close attention, especially in regard to the central subject.

It should be an appropriate size for the subject. We often see situations where the base has been chosen first of all, and the model forced to fit it. On the other hand, bases that are too big are equally bad. A large empty area of water lacks interest. Look at my model of HMS *Hood*, towards the end of this chapter, which I have included as an example of how NOT to make a diorama.

Try to avoid subjects that are illogical, impossible or ludicrous. *Hood* and *Bismarck* slogging it out on the same base, and only a few inches apart. Or two ships close together, in line abreast and going at flank speed. Both captains would be facing courts martial for endangering their ships. Far better to make two nice single ships than an arrangement that, although technically a diorama, is something that strikes the viewer as simply wrong.

A diorama should not be boring

If you have been to a model show or two, you will be sure to have seen what I would describe as 'same old – same old' dioramas. The usual culprits are military vehicle dioramas, but only because these form the majority of dioramas as a whole. Typically, these will have a street corner with the shell of a bombed out building. There will be two or three, usually German, vehicles. And a group of officers will be consulting over a map. It does not matter how well constructed or painted it is, the subject has been done any number of times, and I have seen a hundred of them. I say to myself, 'Oh, yes', and move on to the next.

In a way, ship modelling has the opposite sort of problem. There are a few ships that are such common subjects, that they become boring, and 'same old – same old' subjects. How many *Yamato*s, *Bismarck*s, Iowa Class battleships or Essex Class carriers do you see?

But take that commonly modelled ship, place it into a context that says something, tells a story, or causes you make up your own story, and that *Bismarck* then stands above all those other *Bismarck*s.

A diorama should have suitable number of points of focus

To my mind, when a diorama works well, it does so by having a focus or point of major interest that attracts the eye, and pulls the viewer's attention into the model. Subsidiary points of interest then draw the attention through and around the whole composition.

Imagine you are planning a diorama involving two ships. Let me suggest an aircraft carrier in the process of transferring fuel to one of its escorting destroyers. There is a relationship between the two ships, the act of refuelling. This makes it a logical composition, and the major point of focus will be the fuel pipe connecting the ships, and the knots of crewmen at either end. But there will be other points of focus too. Both ships are underway, and being close together, the officers on both bridges will be concentrating on keeping position. So the

figures you put there will need to emphasise this. Perhaps the sea is a bit choppy, and you will show a variation in roll between the ships. If the ships are in hostile waters, a few fighter planes might be spotted on the carrier's deck, with pilots and deck crew milling around. Flag signals add a touch of colour to the scene. Depending on the size of the scene, you may want to add a couple of other points to draw the attention, but not so many that the eye gets confused, and cannot see the most important features.

A diorama should have enough 'stuff' in it, but not too much

This idea follows on from the previous one, and is closely related to it. If we have a number of points of interest, or activity, in a composition, then our eyes have to be made aware of these, so that the attention can be drawn in. This happens when there is a contrast between the areas of interest and surrounding areas where less is happening.

Do not feel that every square inch of the diorama must be filled with activity, or 'stuff'. There is no need for every piece of deck, or every platform, to have crew figures on them. If it appears as full as a 'Where's Wally?' drawing, then it is all too easy to lose interest in finding what the whole thing is about. Do not be afraid of a bit of empty space, because it makes it easier for the eyes to follow the flow of the diorama.

During the 1970s and 1980s one of the best-known exponents of the military diorama was the Belgian modeller Francois Verlinden. His works appeared in all the magazines, and he published a number of books. Although he was very talented, and his work was cutting edge at the time, there was something I always disliked about his dioramas. He seemed to hate having an empty space, and always tried to fill it with something.

The scene might be, for example, a gun emplacement with an artillery piece. But the base would be evenly scattered with bits and pieces of equipment, large and small. You would see helmets, haversacks, water bottles and gas masks hanging from the gun shield or any other projection. There would be ammunition boxes, open and closed, piled all over the place, with shells resting against the gun trails. Rifles, spades and ranging poles would lean against anything vertical. To my mind, there was just too much stuff, and it was too evenly spread.

Another example of the same thing can be found in the work of my friend Jim Baumann. It is almost heresy to criticise Jim's work, but I have spoken to him about this particular model, and he somewhat agrees with my opinion. I am talking about his Hog Islander diorama, which you will see on page 93. Jim has said to me that he originally planned something very simple, perhaps based around railway rolling stock, but kept being given samples of products from Battlefleet Models, and felt obliged to keep including them. The result is a modelling *tour de force*, but one that lacks a clear main point of focus, and is lessened thereby.

A diorama should tell a story, or illustrate a theme

When the modeller plans a diorama with a well-defined activity at the centre of it, it is likely that he is aware that he is telling a story. Take the idea I described above of the carrier and destroyer. If the vessels are chosen well, we know that they had a relationship at a specific point in history. We can assume that they came into close proximity some short time ago, that the process of refuelling is taking place, and that they are going to separate and take up their normal stations at some point in the near future. There you have it, a story. As long as he understands what he is looking at, the viewer will get the same story, exactly as if it were written in a book. The diorama works because of this.

But there are more subtle ways of storytelling. Some dioramas, such as my HMS *Kent* on page 22, invite the viewer to use their imagination; to ask questions about what is going on, and, in effect, to write their own story. This story will be different for each viewer, or for each time the model is examined. Their story will be different from my story, and even I will interpret the model differently each time I look at it.

You look at the picket boat by the quarterdeck accommodation ladder, and you start to wonder about the people. You start to involve yourself in what you imagine their lives might be about. It may well be that you have no conscious awareness of asking questions or imagining answers, but I have little doubt that it is going on unconsciously. This is why I think that this diorama, which is so simple

that it is almost *not* a diorama, works so well.

Another excellent example, on page XXXX, is by my friend Mike McCabe, and is of the little Argentine aviso *Commandante General Zapiola*, calling in at a scientific station in Tierra del Fuego. This invites one to ask questions about isolation, loneliness, homesickness and the vital importance of human relationships. Although this diorama is only about 4 inches square, it says more to me than most models many times its size.

Ideas for diorama subjects

Let me try and suggest to you some subjects for dioramas which I think might be particularly good. I should like to point out that these represent my taste alone, and you are well within your rights to say, 'Thank you, but no thank you'.

The obvious choice is to take two ships and put them together on the base. But it is vital for a sensible composition that a relationship between the two ships is clearly evident to any viewer. Just having two battleships travelling side by side is not going to cut the mustard, and as I mentioned above, will be ludicrous. But the idea of underway replenishment is another matter entirely, as it shows purpose and human activity.

How about a couple or even a small flotilla of destroyers or submarines moored alongside their depot ship?

Scratchbuilders might be tempted by the accidental ramming of HMS *Victoria* by HMS *Camperdown* in 1893. This would show the consequences of ships being too close together.

Ships in harbour will often have smaller vessels milling around them, going about their business. These could be the ship's own boats, tugs, harbour craft such as lighters, colliers, oilers and victualling craft. There could be a specialist vessel such as a crane ship or barge. Or maybe, in more peaceful and trusting days than those we now live in, even pleasure craft having a nose around the big warships. I call this basic diorama idea 'Dancing in Attendance', and you will see several in this book.

A variation on this idea might be an attack transport ship, lowering its landing craft, which are circling around, waiting to take up formation and head towards the shore.

Harbour and dockside scenes are popular and a source of endless variety. Provided the choice is sensible and not entirely random, ships moored at a quayside have a reason to be close together, and thereby fitting onto a sensibly sized base. You can also have fun making the buildings, cranes, vehicles, locomotives and rolling stock, and then also considering the activity taking place, such as damage repairs, painting the ship's hull, refitting, victualling, loading or unloading cargoes, homecoming, departure, etc. I have an idea for a kit of an Iron Duke Class battleship, during peacetime in the 1920s, with a ball taking place on the quarterdeck, complete with carriages and limousines on the dockside, bringing the guests.

A combat situation is a tempting choice, but be careful, because of the distances involved. It may be best to use only one ship, and look at the combat from a single point of view. For example, take a US destroyer, at full speed and heeling heavily as it executes a tight evasive turn. All of its guns and directors, as well as the attention of every crew member are directed at one point in the sky, from which the viewer is invited to imagine the *kamikaze* attack is coming.

If there is a situation where combat was at extremely close quarters, then this might be a good choice. Two subjects that spring to mind are the crippled destroyer HMS *Glowworm*, trying to ram the German cruiser *Hipper*, and the American destroyer USS *Laffey* as she found herself only a few yards from the battleship *Hiei*.

National pride or sensitivity will play an important part in subject choice, particularly where combat is involved. As a Brit, I have every intention of portraying the obsolete destroyer *Campbeltown*, her decks crowded with khaki commandos, and in the process of changing flags from the German to the White Ensign, heading to a glorious 'suicide' at St Nazaire. Or what about the 'little ships' at Dunkirk, or the death throes of *Ark Royal*?

I have no doubt that American modellers will draw inspiration from their own naval heritage, Pearl Harbor coming immediately to mind, or perhaps USS *Ward*, if there is a wish to keep things simple. Another dramatic idea might be the USS *Birmingham* alongside the crippled *Princeton*. If you want to do the Japanese surrender ceremony on board the USS *Missouri*, it is possible to buy a complete fret of photo-etched figures, including a camera and tripod.

An RNLI lifeboat could be shown rescuing crew from a foundering merchantman in a heavy storm. This might be a fitting tribute to the courageous and unpaid volunteers who man these boats, and who sometimes make the ultimate sacrifice for others.

Although emotion is a human attribute, I believe it is possible for a diorama to portray emotion, without there being any visible human presence at all. If painters and photographers can do it, why can't we? If you manage to imbue the ships with enough personality, they become surrogate humans. Imagine a rotting, derelict wooden pier, perhaps with a tumble down shack on the end or next to it. Tied up alongside are two forgotten tugboats, windows broken, doors and hatches open, paint faded and peeling and rust of various colours on every metal surface. Nobody has trodden their decks for years, and even the ship-breaker doesn't want to know. The only 'friends' these vessels have are each other, and maybe the gulls depositing their guano. The atmosphere of neglect and desolation is heightened by the very absence of any human figure from the scene.

You can find inspiration for similar dioramas in photographs of once-proud warships being broken up after the end of the Second World War.

DIORAMA COMPOSITION

Let us suppose that you have decided what the subject of your diorama is going to be, and that you have chosen the models that you are going to use. I should now like to give you some thoughts on how to make a satisfying composition.

The first consideration ought to be the size and shape of the base. The most important factor deciding this question ought to be the dimensions of the model ships themselves and the size necessary to enclose them without them either seeming cramped by a base that is too small, or lost in one that is too big. The base should not force you to place the models in an awkward position.

We often see dioramas where the base has been chosen before the ships. One of the main culprits is a ready-made picture frame. Let's assume it is intended to take an A4 sized picture. It's just a touch too short to accommodate the 1/350 destroyer that the modeller (not you, I hope) is building. 'But look, if it is put diagonally from corner to corner, it will just fit in.' The result is a ship that is squeezed, or 'shoe-horned' into a space that it does not fit, and there is a triangle of water on either side. However well things have been built, and whatever other items are included in the diorama, there is no hiding the fact that the overall composition has been cobbled together inappropriately.

It is a much better idea to work out your arrangement on paper, decide the exact size and shape of base that you need, and either build your own, or get it custom made. Doing it yourself is not difficult, and I will show you how later on.

Other factors come into play when deciding on base size, such as how it is to be stored and kept safe from damage and dust, or the need to transport it to and from model clubs and shows, and how well it will fit into your car.

When I am making a model that is simply a single waterline ship on a sea base, and not to be considered as a diorama, I make a base that conforms quite closely to the dimensions of the ship. I give myself around 5cm clearance at both bow and stern and on both sides, resulting in a base that can be quite long and narrow, and does not detract attention from the ship itself. The ship is placed exactly along the centreline of the base, parallel to, and equidistant from both sides. The effect that I am aiming for is to give the impression that the ship and a piece of water have simply been 'lifted out of the world'. I think the parallels emphasise this idea. The function of the water is simply to show that the ship is floating, and whether or not it is moving. The focus of attention is the ship and the sea must not detract from this, either by its shape or extent.

When I build a diorama I am doing something entirely different. The base of a diorama is part of the world. The ships are in this bit of world, this microcosm, if you like. The viewer's eye must be drawn into the arrangement and encouraged to move from one part to another, in order to admire every bit of my handiwork. The base has a vital role to play here. It gives sufficient space for the various elements of the diorama to appear as separate entities, but still to have the relationships between each other that I want to show.

Which brings me, at last, to the matter of avoiding parallels and diagonals. It is said that 'Nature abhors a straight line'. This is not entirely true; think of the sides of a crystal or the path that a ray of light follows. But in general terms, straight lines are a human invention; the natural world prefers a degree of irregularity. If you include a bit of irregularity in your diorama design, this will mimic the real world to some extent.

If you avoid placing the various elements so that they are parallel to the edges of the base, or on the exact centre line or diagonal, and try to have them so that they are a touch skewed, off-centre, etc, you will break up the base into areas that are of varying sizes and shapes. This will encourage the eye to move around the scene from one part to another and always find something interesting. On the other hand, too much regularity in the way that things are set out will restrict the way the eye moves and cause it to just go back and forth. Admittedly, some things will need to be parallel, such as a ship tied up alongside a quay, or two ships that are moving side by side in a refuelling scene. But by twisting the whole arrangement around, just by a small amount, within the confines of the base you will achieve a much greater sense of life.

I spoke earlier about having a number of 'points of focus' in a diorama. These are areas in the composition which should be of interest to the viewer, and to which his attention should be drawn. It might seem obvious to place the point of major interest right in the centre of the composition, because this is where the attention would tend to go first of all. If you do this, the attention will certainly go to that point of interest, but it will tend to stay there, be reluctant to move away, and the whole arrangement will seem rather static, bland and unexciting.

Place the main points of focus, and I hope you will have two or three of them, away from the centre of the base, although not right at the edges, either. What will then happen is that the eye will start off in the centre, be drawn away, first to one point of focus and then another, perhaps round in a circle and then back again. This creates what I would describe as a 'tension' between the areas of interest. By this, I do not mean the sense of anticipation, excitement and anxiety that is built up

▲ This photo and the next are intended to illustrate the idea of avoiding parallels and diagonals. The three hulls represent two destroyers moored at a single buoy, and another approaching to tie up alongside them. A boat is taking the picking up rope to the buoy. Here the stationary ships are parallel to the sides of the base, and the moving one is only very slightly skewed. I think the composition looks rather static and bland

▲ I have now made the base slightly wider from front to rear. This gives me the space to put an angle between the moored destroyers and the edge of the base, and also to increase the angle that the single destroyer is at. I am assuming that it has its engines idling, and that it is, in fact, practically stationary. I think that this arrangement is more satisfactory as the eye finds the angles more exciting, and in the finished scene would be encouraged to flit around as though it were on a pinball machine.

in a James Bond film. Tension in a diorama, or any kind of picture, is that sensation you get when you realise that your attention is being pulled from one thing to another and back again, and so on. You are able to easily identify those parts of the composition that are important without being confused by lots of trivia, the only function of which is to fill up empty spaces.

It is very likely that some dioramas that you make will have smaller vessels or boats arranged around, or in relationship to a larger one. In general it is a good idea to try to have the smaller craft pointing or moving towards the centre of the composition, rather than towards the edges. The viewer's eye will tend to follow the direction of travel of these craft and will be drawn into the diorama.

But, as with many rules, this can be broken with good effect. Suppose the diorama has a theme of 'Farewell' or 'Departure'. A small craft moving away, perhaps with crewmen waving to it from the ship, will show this idea quite well.

As I write this, it occurs to me that in my diorama of the armoured cruiser HMS *Cumberland*

the positioning of the two barges goes against this advice. So I've put some photos of it here to show you. Both are pointing outwards, towards the edges of the diorama. With regards to the one that is underway, this is because I wanted to show the starboard side of the craft, in order to demonstrate the distinctive rig of the spritsail barge. The diagonal sprit supporting the mainsail is always on the starboard side of the sail. In retrospect, I might have done better to have the barge in the rear left corner, still sailing towards the right, and turned the cruiser round the other way, and on the opposite diagonal, with the bows towards the front left. To this one I hold my hands up, 'Guilty as charged, your Honour.'

The reason for the positioning of the barge at the ship's quarterdeck is less avoidable. I reckoned that if a sailing craft were to approach the ship's quarter from astern, it would run the risk of catching its rigging on the casemate 6 inch guns. I also wanted to show off the elegant and colourfully painted transom stern. So in this second case there is logic for breaking the rule.

▲ HMS *Cumberland* showing both barges apparently pointing the wrong way

◄ With the mainsail brailed up on this barge, the sprit is obvious. But you can also see how the rigging would have got entangled with the guns if it had tried to approach from astern

▶ The barge by the cruiser's bow. This is actually taken from the rear of the diorama. The interesting sprit is on the other side of the sail, and would be visible when viewed from the front

▼ How NOT to plan a diorama. I made this model of HMS *Hood* around the year 2000. It won the ship diorama class at Telford. I was surprised, and chuffed to ninepence at the time, but I no longer think I deserved it. The base is far too big, resulting in a vast expanse of empty water, which is distracting to the eye by the very fact that there is nothing in it. The decks look almost void of any activity, and that's true, there is almost nothing happening. The main focus of attention is not at the dead centre, which would be bad, but it is right at the stern, which is actually worse

▲ Admiral Holland being welcomed on board the ship, prior to her last, tragic sortie. Apart from a few men on the foredeck, fiddling with the capstan, and something happening around one of the 4 inch mountings, this is just about the only activity in the diorama. Do you know what I think? 'BORING!

▲ I had just finished writing a section about storytelling in dioramas when, by a spooky coincidence, I discovered photos of this diorama on the Internet. It is called 'Fairy Tale of the River', by Katarzyna Manikowska, from Poland. It is a card model of an oil tanker from the River Volga. It is sailing past the Hut of Baba Yaga. She is a witch from Eastern European folklore, and her hut walks around on chicken's legs. She has mounted everything not on a conventional base, but on a length of driftwood. This adds to the dreamlike quality of the composition. Or maybe it's more of a nightmare! Whatever, I think it is storytelling of the first order. (THIS PHOTO AND THE FOLLOWING THREE BY KATARZYNA MANIKOWSKA)

◄ And here you see how she is starting to build up the diorama as a whimsical piece of fantasy. Using the driftwood as a base, she is not being so hidebound by the conventional ideas of 'realism' as most of the rest of us. Quite honestly, I love it!

▲ Another of Katarzyna's dioramas. You can tell exactly what the story is here. This is a card model as well. They are very popular in Germany and Eastern Europe. They are available with a vast variety of subjects. Ships are generally 1/200 or 1/250 scale, and some are of the most mind-boggling complexity.

◀ And a final example of storytelling from Katarzyna. This is 1/350, and the whole thing is only about 5cm across. The fisherman is trying to catch an impossibly big fish, bigger than the boat itself. You know exactly what is going to happen here. The fish will get off the hook, the guys will spend a drunken evening in the quayside bar, and absolutely nobody will believe a word of their story of 'the one that got away!' This is not a truly realistic story or situation. But if it makes you smile, then it matters not one iota!

CHAPTER 2

'DANCING IN ATTENDANCE'

I should like to suggest that you look at some photos of ships at anchor. Perhaps go onto www.navsource.org and look at images from the late nineteenth and first half of the twentieth centuries. Very often you will see the larger ships with smaller vessels and boats milling around.

These may be the ship's own boats. Or they could be harbour craft of various types, oilers and colliers, victualing craft, barges and lighters, tugs, pilots' launches or even private yachts in earlier times.

Each of these smaller craft has its own purpose *vis-à-vis* the larger one: transporting officers and men, loading fuel and supplies, off-loading junk and rubbish, pushing or pulling the ship. The ship's own boats may be simply tied up to the boat booms, waiting to be used.

The depiction of this kind of scene is the purpose of what I consider to be the simplest of ship dioramas. I give it the generic title 'Dancing in Attendance'. It may not be a complex idea, but this does not prevent it from being a remarkably effective form of diorama. In its most basic form it may not be big and brash enough to impress judges at a big competition, but that is not my intention. What I want to do is to put a model ship into context and bring it to life, and an arrangement where there is just one or two small boats having a purposeful relationship with the main vessel can do this superbly.

Look at the pictures on page 22 below. These show my model of the armoured cruiser HMS *Kent* and will illustrate this point.

The ship is at anchor. The port boat boom is rigged and two of the ship's boats are moored to it. A steam launch is by the accommodation ladder hanging from the quarterdeck and a few people are fussing around at the top of the ladder.

This is the 'dancing in attendance' idea stripped down to its absolute fundamentals. It is so stripped down that it would turn no heads in the diorama classes of most large competitions. In fact, it has been entered in single ship classes. Nevertheless, as

an example of a bit of animation being put into a model, it is my sincere opinion that it works very well indeed. Even though it was a number of years ago that I built this model, it remains one of my favourites.

Let's examine what happens when we look at the model. The viewer's eye is taken on a journey. It is first drawn to the steam launch and the accommodation ladder. It is as though we are entering the model by climbing the ladder, just as the officer has done. This area forms one of the main foci of interest. Attention can then move to the mainmast. With its intricate rigging, this is another major focus of interest. We then go along the main deck, past boats on the skid beams and davits, and the funnels with their guys. These are secondary foci of interest. We arrive at the bridge area. This is the second major focus. There is the foremast, again with rigging and the signal flags giving a touch of colour, and activity happening on the bridge. From the bridge, attention can go to the foredeck, or alternatively, via the men cleaning the 6-pounder gun, to the boat boom, and thence back to the steam launch.

A successful diorama will be telling a story to the viewer. This diorama is telling a story, but I don't know what it is. Maybe you know better? The areas of main interest are where the viewer finds himself asking questions about what is going on in the model, and his imagination is then called into play in order to answer them. You look at the quarterdeck and say to yourself: 'Who is that, coming on board?', 'Where has he come from?', 'Who is he going to see?', 'What news or orders has he brought?', 'Will they soon be sailing away?' Or you will look at the flag signals and ask to whom they are directed and what they are saying. And I would have to reply, in all honesty, that I don't know the answer to that one either. D-R-M are simply my father-in-law's initials. As a signal it could mean anything from 'Party tonight, bring your own booze' to 'The Bosun's down with the measles!'

▼ HMS *Kent*

▲ HMS *Kent*. Bridge and foremast

▲ HMS *Kent*. Steam launch at the quarterdeck

▲ If this chapter is called 'Dancing in Attendance' then this diorama must be the Royal Ballet. This is Jim Baumann's model of the French battleship *Henri IV*. Just look at all the pleasure craft and fishing boats swirling around. The whole thing bewitches the eye. Being a sailor, Jim has ensured that all the sails are set correctly for the direction that he has decided the wind is blowing. (PHOTO BY JIM BAUMANN)

▲ I'm not sure what Jim has done with the lighting in this photo. Maybe he lowered the light levels deliberately, or maybe not. But the effect is to make it look like one of those seventeenth century Dutch paintings with boats in a storm. You cannot deny that it is extremely atmospheric. (PHOTO BY JIM BAUMANN)

▲ A vaguely similar idea, but not so well executed. This is my model of the USS *Chicago* with boats around her. Jim had often said he would like to have one of my models in his collection, so I hoisted his daughter's initials in signal flags, and this one is now sitting in one of his display cabinets

▼ This shows the overall layout. The *Chicago* is not on the centre line of the base and not parallel to the sides. Neither is it on the exact diagonal. It is positioned slightly towards the back of the base. This gives room in the water for the steam launch and the sailing boat not to feel crowded and have their own individual identities

MAKING A BASE

Before I go any further into the construction of a particular diorama, I think this would be a good point to describe the processes involved in making your own base, as this is something that all dioramas are going to need.

If you are going to be picky about the size of base you want to have, it tends to follow that ready-made bases are not going to be suitable. It is possible to get bases custom-made to your exact specifications, but it is actually not too difficult to make your own. I have always done so; I only rarely use commercial bases, and have never had one specially made.

My bases are made from MDF, usually 4mm thick, and they are surrounded with a frame cut from picture frame moulding, which I buy in 2.4 metre lengths, and I cut my own joints using a small mitre box.

I cut the moulding in an unusual and specific way. If you take a conventional picture frame and place it on the table face up, you will notice that the rebate that takes the glass, picture and backing is on the back, or rather the bottom as you are now looking at it. If you were to imagine the glass as the sea surface and the model is floating in it, then the frame ends up being raised above the sea. To my mind this makes the ship look as though it is floating in a swimming pool.

So what I do is to turn the moulding outwards by 90° so that the rebate is brought to the front inner edge of the frame. The sheet of MDF is now raised up so that the surface of the sea appears to be on top of the frame, and the ship is not so constrained.

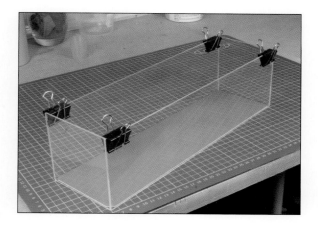

▲ I am making a base and case for my next project, HMS *Agincourt* in 1/700 scale. I wanted the size of the sea to be fourteen inches long by four inches wide. I think it's easier to cut wood to fit exactly into and around an acrylic case, than it is to cut acrylic sheet, or order it, such that the resulting case will fit neatly. So I ordered 2mm thick acrylic first of all, and had it delivered ready cut to size, bearing in mind the need to have an allowance for the butt joints at the corners. You can see that I am assembling the case around a piece of cardboard of the appropriate size, to keep the ends from slipping too far inside, and the corners square. The bulldog clips are there to do the same at the top, being positioned exactly 2mm from the end of each side piece. The edges have been sanded smooth and polished where necessary so that they will glue well without the joints being too obtrusive. I have used a solvent cement called Evo-Plas Tensol 12, which is specifically intended for plastics like this, and obtained from the company that supplied the acrylic

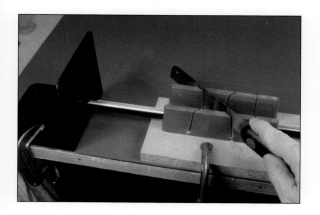

◀ Using the mitre box to cut 45° angles. The mitre box is clamped firmly to the worktop. The metal bookend from IKEA or a similar emporium is also clamped at an appropriate distance to act as a stop, so that I can cut pieces of moulding that are identical lengths. I am using a sharp dovetail saw. Incidentally, this one is a saw that cuts on the 'pull' stroke, in Japanese fashion, and I find it very good. I have posed this picture for the camera. If I were actually cutting, I would be holding the moulding in place with my left hand, and that would be all you could see. I'm sure I have a most elegant left hand, but it is hardly relevant to the book

◀ The acrylic case has had its top glued on and is now reasonably rigid. I measured the lengths of moulding directly from the case, so that the frame would fit snugly around it but still be easy to remove. A baseboard of MDF was cut to the same size as the cardboard in the first photo, and this has been glued into the rebate in the frame. You have now formed a slot into which the case will neatly fit

Two points require to be made about this process. First, the moulding has to be chosen carefully so that it will still look attractive around the base when it is turned outwards like this. Secondly, you have to cut the mitres yourself, not get a picture framer to do it for you. Commercial framers use guillotines rather than saws, and if the moulding is put into the machine in what is regarded as the 'wrong' way it gets crushed instead of cut cleanly.

Before now I have just kept my models in a glass fronted cabinet to protect them from dust and damage. This protection is only partial; in particular static electrical build-up still attracts dust. So I have recently decided to include an integral acrylic case with my bases, and I shall show you how to do this too.

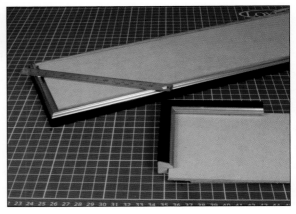

▲ I may not have explained the reason for turning the moulding through 90° entirely clearly, so this photo should make the point. In the front I have cut the moulding in the normal orientation that you would use to frame a picture. The position of the rebate causes the frame to sit proud of the base, just like, as I said earlier, a swimming pool. At the rear is the base as I intended. Turning the moulding brings the rebate to the top and the base is now level with the top of the frame. You can see that there is no gap under the ruler. I really think this is a much superior way of going about it. It is just that you have to do it all yourself rather than paying a picture framer. If you don't count the time spent building the acrylic case, it takes less than an hour to make a typical base, so it is not only cheaper than having it made for you, it is probably also quicker, unless you live over a framer's shop!

USS LANGLEY

I am going to illustrate the process of constructing a 'Dancing in Attendance' diorama with my model of the USS *Langley*, the US Navy's first aircraft carrier. It uses the 1/700 resin kit from Loose Cannon, and is combined with the yard oiler and garbage lighter from Battlefleet Models and some dockyard barges that I scratchbuilt. You might say that the theme is one of 'In One Side & Out The Other', with the oiler representing the 'in' and the barges and garbage lighter the 'out'. I know it's a fairly tenuous thought, but feel free to take it or leave it.

I love the little harbour craft that are produced by Battlefleet. They may not be the most detailed or advanced kits on the market, but they are incredibly useful for the diorama builder. You only need to place one or two around a more major vessel, bearing in mind that the smaller vessels have to be doing something, and you are on your way to an instant diorama. Add some mooring ropes to show

▼ Here we see some of the work that I did on *Langley*'s hull. The shape of the parts is only approximate, and a lot of them need to be defined much better. Detail is crude, lacking, or inaccurate. The hatches on the 'hangar deck' were ground away and replaced with a thinner sheet of plasticard, engraved to represent the hinged plates that gave access to the interior of the ship. The resin bulwarks were cut away and plastic replacements fitted. A coat of grey primer showed up areas of the hull surface that were uneven and required filling and

rubbing down, as you can see. All the deckhouses on the after end of the ship had unsightly raised window details trimmed off. They were then covered with five thou plasticard with rather more accurate, square window openings cut into them. Thanks to Peter Van Buren for showing where the windows ought to be. I worked on the assumption that his model was rather more accurate. It also gave me some indication of the arrangement of the trunking to the folding funnels, which ran across the deck. Talk about Health & Safety!

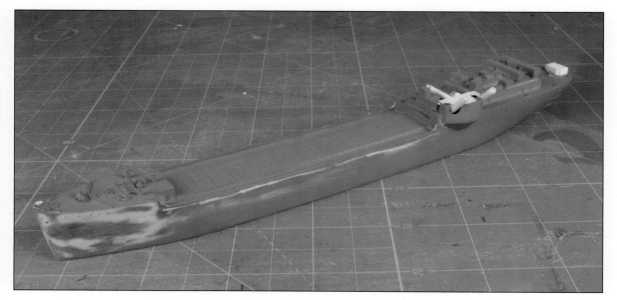

that the vessels have a definite relationship and some crew figures communicating with each other, and there you are. You can win a prize.

Really that is all that I have done with this diorama. There has been no complicated quayside or buildings to construct. Just one large ship and a few little ones.

The small craft that are doing the dancing in attendance, although they are subsidiary to the main vessel in real life, are not mere bit players in the diorama. It is they that bring it to life. They are every bit as important as the large ship. You could even say that they are more important. They are what make the diorama. Without them you would be looking at a model of a single ship.

When you look at the diorama, your eyes are drawn into it by way of the little vessels. For this reason it is important to take just as much care in making and finishing them as you would with the main vessel.

So let's get on and build the model.

I bought the Loose Cannon *Langley* in 2008, at the IPMS US Nationals. There was a very nicely done example of the kit on the competition table, so I knew that it was possible to get a good result. But I didn't realise just how much work this kit would take. Loose Cannon choose some very interesting subjects, and are to be commended for this. Many ships would not appear in kit form were it not for Loose Cannon.

But unfortunately, they take a great deal of effort to bring the detail, and even the shapes of basic structures up to scratch.

I did not have a good set of drawings of the *Langley*, although I believe they are commercially

▼ When you open the box for this kit, the thing that strikes you first is the large sheet of photo-etch for all the girders that support the flight deck. It does not have quite the finesse that we have come to expect from Gold Medal or White Ensign, but the thicker brass folds very easily, and certainly looks the business. But looks can be deceiving, and when I began dry fitting everything onto the ship, I discovered that it was too long for the hull. Or maybe the hull master had been built without allowing for the resin shrinking. Every longitudinal component (those marked with a letter on the photo) had to be slightly trimmed at both ends in order for the transverse members to sit at the correct positions along the hull. Towards the stern even more drastic surgery was needed. The rivet counters, or perhaps the diagonal girder counters, will pull me up for it, but I don't care. It looks OK. The bridge, which can be see nestling under the girders at the break of the fo'c'sle, was built from plastic card and strip, as the kit part was awful, being built up from just vague shapes and none of them square. I don't know how accurate my interpretation is, but it is not terribly visible on the completed model

available. For reference I used photos in books and on the web, such as are found on Navsource and some extremely scrappy little drawings in Whitely's book on aircraft carriers. I also drew inspiration from Peter Van Buren's 1/350 model of the ship, and from photos of a builder's model that appeared on the Steel Navy website, but which seems to differ from the photographic records in many ways, and to be something of an approximation to the appearance of the original ship.

◀ This is the base for the model. It has been made much earlier in the process than is my usual practice, but if you are working out the precise positions for the various vessels, you need to know the size and shape of the base you will use. A piece of 6mm MDF forms the surface, and some thick and rough surfaced watercolour paper glued on top. I normally glue the hull of the model directly to the paper, but the bottom of the *Langley*'s hull was uneven, and the cut-out helped to hide this

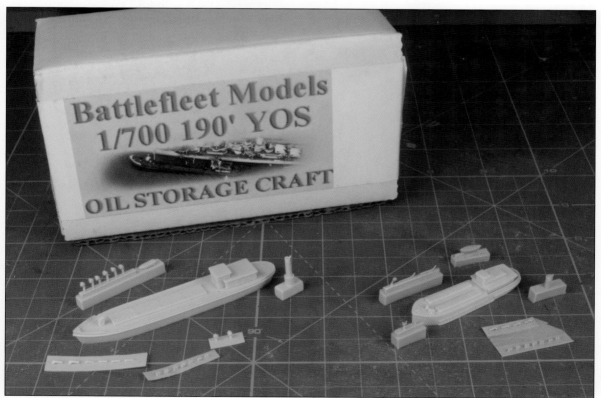

▲ These are the Battlefleet kits. They are very simple products, and to me some of the shapes look a little 'stereotyped', but they look the business as the bustling little handmaids of the big ships. I particularly like the garbage lighter, with its hatches in the side of the hull. It reminds me of a smaller and dumpier version of a ship that is sometimes seen sailing in the River Clyde, loaded down to the gunwales as it goes downstream and high in the water as it returns, having discharged its load of processed sewage into the sea somewhere near Ailsa Craig! I'm sorry, that was too much information, wasn't it?

▶ These are plastic masters that I made for resin casting. They represent a selection of the barges that were used around US Navy dockyards. The basic hull dimensions were obtained from Navsource, and other visual details found on the same website and also in the background of photos in books by Squadron

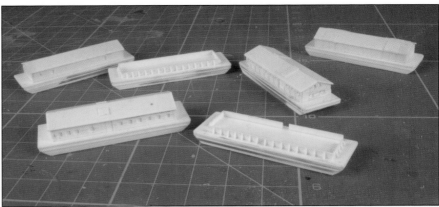

and Classic Warships Publishing. I do not claim that they are totally accurate. The hulls are made from two pieces of sixty or eighty thou plasticard glued together and cut to size. The superstructure is built from engraved plasticard to replicate corrugated steel sheeting. The window cut outs are backed with more

plastic. Rubbing strakes and other details are made from Evergreen strip. After I had made a silicone rubber mould for my own use, and cast copies in resin, I sent the masters off to Harry Abbott of Battlefleet Models, for his own use. He is producing and selling copies with my blessing

▲ Here you see the arrangement that I came up with for the major components of the diorama. As in the *Chicago* diorama, the *Langley* is slightly towards the back of the composition. This means I can have three craft in front and one behind without it looking odd. The two rectangular barges occupy the wide end of the larger triangle that has been formed in the base.

This is because, sitting side by side, they are wider than either the oiler or the garbage lighter. The barges and the garbage lighter, being tied up alongside the *Langley*, have to be parallel to her, but the oiler is at a bit of an angle, and this implies movement and 'life'. When complete, there will be some work boats about the place, and these will tend to break up the straight lines

▶ The kit included a wooden flight deck. It is a personal choice, but I do not like the current trend for wooden decks, as the grain of natural wood looks out of place on a model. I much prefer to see a good paint job on a plastic or resin deck. Although this deck had been laser-cut to give fine transverse planking, the grain of the wood was running fore and aft, which was entirely wrong.

So, using the wood deck as a pattern, I made a replacement out of scribed plastic card. But when I came to fit it, I found that the wooden deck had the elevator engraved in the wrong place, right over one of the transverse girders. So what you see here is replacement number two. I am quite pleased with the netting at the edge of the flight deck. I made this from a pair of nylon tights, which I stole from my long-suffering wife. I stretched them by placing an open box inside them, and then painted diluted PVA glue onto the fabric. I blew vigorously onto it to burst all the bubbles in the holes. When dry, the fabric was stiff and could be cut into strips that do not fray and look much more like rope netting than photo-etch does

▲ Here you can see the yard craft completed and painted. The oiler has had pipes and valves put along and across the deck, and some hatches, using photos from *United States Navy Destroyers of World War II* by John C Reilly as guidance. The garbage lighter has had the deck hatches opened up on one side and the interior hollowed out. Metal masts have been added to both vessels, along with photo-etched railings, davits, etc. The colour scheme for all four craft is primarily black, but I actually painted them in a very dark grey.

These were working boats, and proudly grimy. So, following the techniques that I showed in my previous book, I used artist's oil paints to apply filters, pin-washes, vertical streaking, horizontal scratches and scuff marks, dry-brushing, etc. The use of the colour known as burnt umber is especially useful for grime and rust, which is often depicted in hues that I consider too bright and orangey. The overall effect is something that is fundamentally black, but with a lot of visual texture or variety

And now here are a few photos of the completed diorama. If you are wondering about the aircraft on the flight deck, I must make a confession. The kit included some P-40 *Tomahawks*, rather than biplanes. Rather than mess around trying to scratch-build them I just found some Japanese ones in the spares box and trimmed the tail fins to make them look rather squarer and American. Rivet counters, leave me alone!

I also tried to mark lines along the hull in pencil to imitate the plating. This was not very successful, and in retrospect I would have been better to have thought ahead and used strips of Bare Metal Foil.

CHAPTER 3

'TWO'S COMPANY, THREE'S A CROWD'

This chapter is about planning and making dioramas containing more than one major vessel. This sounds like a logical step on from the 'dancing in attendance' theme, but it is a step that is fraught with danger.

On a number of occasions I have seen people writing things on the Internet along the lines of, 'I've just bought 1/350 kits of *Yamato* and *Nagato*. I think I'll make a diorama out of them.' It doesn't take a lot of imagination to see what a disaster the result will be.

How many examples have we all seen where two large ships are placed side by side on a single base, and shown steaming at full speed. I know I've said this earlier in the book, but it is a point worth making again. If you are going to place two vessels close together, then there has to be a logical reason for them to be together, and also to be doing whatever is being shown.

For reasons of safety, ships underway generally keep a reasonable distance between each other, far more than would make for an artistically satisfying model. So arrangements like this are best avoided. It does not matter how perfectly the two ships have been built or painted, or how wonderful the sea effect is, placing them together in close proximity without logical reason makes for a thoroughly bad 'diorama'. I put the inverted commas in deliberately. Let them be two beautifully made single ships instead.

Of course, there are certain circumstances when ships do come close together while moving. Usually these will be very controlled. The main one that comes to mind is that of underway replenishment or refuelling, or alternatively transferring the mail or crew members on a bosun's chair. Or one ship could be offering assistance to another that has been damaged, or is otherwise in distress.

The possible result of the 'bad diorama' idea is another 'reason' for ships to be close together. Collision. The two ideas may only be separated by a few seconds of time in the real world, but a collision

would make an entirely suitable and exciting subject for a diorama. Accidents have always happened at sea, and probably always will. The deliberate version of a collision, ramming as part of combat could also be shown. It does not often happen, but there are a number of famous incidents.

Let's leave ships travelling at speed for a while and consider those that are stationary, moored or anchored, or moving very slowly. Here we have much greater opportunity to use our imagination in ways that are potentially realistic. Ships may share the same mooring buoy, and be side by side, or be tied up to the same quay. A group of smaller vessels may be tied up alongside their depot ship. A ship may be manoeuvring slowly past other ships in harbour. Ships may be transferring cargoes or taking on stores. And ships in these situations may be receiving assistance from tugs and harbour craft.

The essential difference between the 'steaming together at full speed' idea and all these others that I have suggested is that in my 'good' ideas there is a sensible and understandable relationship between the ships. The first has no real relationship, just reluctance on the part of the modeller to cut a large piece of plywood into two narrow rectangles, on the grounds that bigger must be better.

I am sincerely sorry if the foregoing sounds as though it is a bit of a 'rant', but one of the main reasons that I decided to write this book is that I have seen far too many 'steaming together at full speed' dioramas at model shows or on the Internet.

PLANNING YOUR DIORAMA

The question that goes along with the theme of the diorama is that of what individual ships, or types of ships, to depict. It is not enough to just take two or more kits from your stash and say, 'That'll do.'

You are placing two vessels in the same place and time. Are the models appropriate for that particular place and time? Model companies will often produce a series of kits to represent different ships of the same class. But they will have a variety of fits to demonstrate the changes that happened over the course of their careers. So you do not want to end up putting a ship in a 1942 configuration with 'Chicago pianos' and a few 20mm guns next to a late war version, bristling with quad 40mm guns and sprouting radar aerials all over the place. Even worse would be to have a ship that has just emerged from her late war refit, and put her on the same base as a ship that had been sunk the previous year.

The same thing holds true for colour schemes. It is tempting to show off the diversity of camouflage patterns worn by ships, but make sure that, given the dates of introduction and withdrawal, they could have conceivably appeared on ships next to each other.

Not just time, but also place. Did the service histories of the ships mean that they served in totally different theatres of war, and could never have met? A lot of such information is available on the Internet and can easily be checked.

Smaller ships, such as destroyers and escort vessels, served in flotillas or squadrons, and can be shown in company with a fair degree of conviction. A Task Force, with large vessels and their protective screen of smaller ships, puts a variety of different types of ships into the same area of sea at the same time. The composition of these Task Forces is simply verified.

If you are using a photograph to give you inspiration, then you have proof of proximity between ships, provided they are accurately identified.

So you have chosen your ships, worked out the theme or activity that you will depict, and convinced yourself that it could look both realistic and artistically satisfying on a base of reasonable dimensions. Before you start building the models, I hope you will have given due consideration to how they will be positioned on the base, and that you will follow my advice regarding parallels and diagonals.

As I mentioned in the chapter 'Models in Context', the empty areas between the main elements of the diorama have a function to perform as well. Do not be too afraid of them. Unless they are very large and distracting, in which case you have not thought your diorama through fully, they do not need to be filled up with 'stuff'.

If you have been careful in composing your ships within a base of suitable proportions, you will have areas of sea that give the ships 'elbow room' without being so large that they intrude too much on the attention. But with the best will in the world you may end up with a corner that has nothing in it, but at the same time looks too big. Its emptiness demands that something be put into it in order to regain a sense of balance in the composition. So you may want to add a small extra element, a boat, for example.

Something of this kind may well be an afterthought, but don't treat it as *just* an afterthought. Small it may be, but it will be one of those little things that will be easily noticed, out in the open and not hidden. Lavish a bit of care on it. Make sure that the hull is sanded down to a realistic waterline. Let the crew figures be doing what they ought to; someone on the tiller, rowers rowing with oars parallel on each side of the boat, maybe a man standing on the bow with a boathook. Or perhaps it is a sailing boat, for which you can make sails from cigarette paper. In that case, have you considered the direction that the wind is blowing in the diorama as a whole? Which way are the flags flying on the other ships? How should the sails be set, and should the boat be heeling much?

As well as being a little jewel to be admired, a small boat like this can add a certain dynamic element to the composition. The eye will naturally tend to follow the direction that the boat is travelling. So if the boat is shown as moving towards one of the major ships, or towards the centre of the diorama, rather than away from it, it will help to draw the viewer's attention towards what is really important.

As I have mentioned before, the whole point of a diorama with two or more large vessels is to show some kind of relationship or interaction between them. The diorama must show this, and the viewer must be able to get the gist of it without having it pointed out. Otherwise, it is just two ships on a base.

This interaction, whatever it may be, should be the central point of focus of the diorama. Even though it is the most important part, it is best if it is placed away from the exact centre. Position it somewhat to one side, and back or forwards a bit. As I mentioned in the first chapter, this enables the eye to be drawn around the arrangement more readily, rather than being stuck in the centre. It can be balanced by other secondary foci of interest.

FIGURES

When you start to put figures on a model, it really begins to come to life. Never forget that sailors are very proud of the ships they serve on, no matter how humble. It is like a large family, or a small town. Attention is immediately drawn to the little men, and the imagination starts to give them personalities and gets involved with them. Use the figures to illustrate or emphasise the activities that are taking place on board. But do not use them simply to fill up empty space.

I have seen many otherwise excellent models that are rather spoiled by indiscriminate or careless use of figures. They are placed on every available piece of deck and on every platform. Often they are standing alone in the middle of an empty deck, as though they do not know what they are doing. For the same reason that I do not like to see excessive amounts of 'stuff', a large number of crew figures spread around too evenly distracts from what is important in the diorama.

Before I glue any figure onto the deck of a ship model I always ask myself why he is going to be in that particular place and what it is that he is supposed to be doing. I also try to put most of the figures in groups, rather than singly. I feel that this makes them much more significant. They will be talking to each other, engaged in some common purpose, and you will find out their stories. The sort of general activities may be trivial or very general, walking from point A to point B, officers chatting on the quarterdeck or ratings smoking by the rail. If a figure is walking, I try to make it clear where he has come from and where he is going to. Often it is going to be to join another group of men. I will always have figures on the bridge. Probably someone will be hoisting a flag signal (I usually spell out someone's initials on my ships using flags!) Other groups may be carrying out maintenance on pieces of equipment, cleaning the deck, moving stores or checking the mooring hawsers. I never feel the need to populate every bit of deck, and I will have many of the platforms empty. I believe that a relatively small number of figures, carefully arranged, can be much more interesting and visually satisfying.

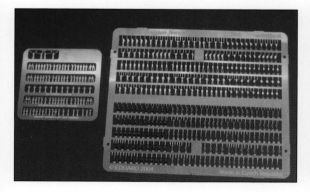

▲ 1/700 scale photo-etched figures. On the left is a fret from Gold Medal and on the right a ready-painted one from Eduard. The Eduard fret offers much better value for money, but I'm not convinced by the bright colours. They need both darkening and toning down. The positions are stereotyped. I do not think that such a high proportion of the crew would be standing with arms in the air or saluting

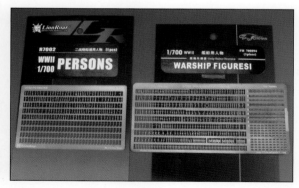

▲ I much prefer these frets from Lion Roar and Flyhawk. There is a greater variety of realistic postures. The bottom four rows on the Lion Roar fret are figures that have arms and legs that are designed to be bent to any position you want, which is a very useful development

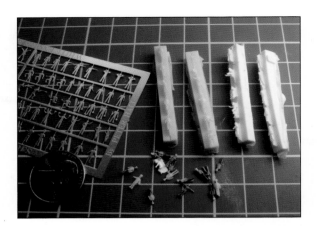

◀ 1/350 scale figures. The photo-etched fret from White Ensign is one of their oldest, and no longer cuts the mustard. The resin figures from L'Arsenal are nicely three dimensional but have relatively few postures. They are fiddly to trim off the moulding blocks and result in quite a few amputations and decapitations, but they are cheap enough that you can populate a battleship without breaking the bank. At the time of writing, some highly detailed castings from a firm called North Star are becoming available. I have not yet been able to see them, but I expect that they will probably be too expensive to crew anything larger than a destroyer

▶ This is my diorama of the battlecruiser HMS *Tiger*, using the Combrig 1/700 kit. In his book *British Battleships*, Oscar Parkes relates how sailors would row for miles to look at her. I postulated that soon after her commissioning, Clyde paddle-steamers might take a detour, or even be chartered to have a nose around. This gives me a good reason for the two vessels to be close together.

"We a' gang doon the watter, tae see that splendid cat' HMS TIGER ON THE CLYDE, 1914

◀ The paddle steamer is scratch-built. I found plans for one called *Redgauntlet* in a copy of *Model Shipwright*, and reduced them in size to 1/700. But I regard it as simply a generic steamer, representative of the hundreds that plied their trade around the Clyde and Argyll coasts. It is quite a basic construction with a wooden hull and plasticard. This is one of those occasions when I am glad of those figures with their arms raised!

This is a diorama by Dr György Pék, from Hungary. It shows the carrier HMS *Invincible*, the destroyer HMS *Sheffield* and the frigate HMS *Brilliant* departing for the Falklands War. As the ships are moving slowly, with the crews at the deck edges, and parading, as it were, for the cheering public, I think that it is reasonable for them to be shown close together. I think that György has used a bit of artistic licence, though, but not nearly enough to take us out of the realms of reality. (PHOTOS BY GYÖRGY PÉK)

György is an ophthalmic surgeon, and it shows in the quality and precision of his modelling. Even the professional photos he has had taken do not do justice to his detail. Just enjoy!

◀ Refuelling at sea is a very suitable diorama subject. Peter Fulgoney's example showing the carrier HMS *Biter* and the destroyer HMS *Obdurate* is particularly attractive. The fact that both ships sport camouflage schemes using the same colours makes for an extremely coherent composition. (PHOTO BY PETER FULGONEY)

▶ This is another very small diorama that I built for the book. It is so simple and does not introduce any significant techniques, so I do not think it warrants its own build feature. It is the Gleaves Class destroyer USS *Monssen*, being nudged into the channel by a tugboat. I was inspired by a photo of the tug *Hoga* pushing a four-piper destroyer at Pearl Harbor.

▲ The tugboat in close up. It isn't by any means an Earth-shattering piece of modelling, but it doesn't have to be. I think it has a certain charm, anyway

 The signal flags are J-H-S, for James Harvey Shacklock, my grandfather. The figures are pre-painted Eduard ones. Even with a dark wash to tone down the colours they look far too bright to my eyes. It may just be a trick of the intense photographic light, but I think not

'WE'RE ALL IN THE BLACK GANG, TODAY'

I have always found the process of loading coal onto a capital ship to be a fascinating idea. Imagine this. Every week or two, the whole ship's company would be employed shovelling coal into sacks, hoisting them aboard, dragging them along the deck and tipping the contents into the bunkers. In some places it might be necessary to carry sacks or baskets of coal on the shoulders, up the gangplanks from quayside onto the ship. The work would go on without break all day and into the night. Morale would be kept up by the ship's band playing stirring music. Everyone would be uniformly filthy and unrecognisable. They would have earned temporary membership of the 'Black Gang', a term usually applied to the stokers and engineers, whose job was to deal with the boilers and engines. And after it was completed, the decks would have to be scrubbed clean of traces of coal dust. I am amazed that wooden decks were not permanently black from ground-in grime. If the ship was sailing a lot, then the whole thing would have to be gone through again only a week or so later.

▼ This is the *Indomitable*. Like all of Combrig's more recent kits, it is highly and delicately detailed, and has a multitude of parts. It was one of the first of their kits to include a sheet of photo-etched parts, albeit rather small compared to most major manufacturers. It has cast resin rods for the masts, yards and torpedo net booms. These are neither strong enough nor stiff enough to do the job, and I replaced them all with brass rod or stainless steel from acupuncture needles. Notice the way the *en echelon* 12 inch gun turrets are turned across the deck. This is to ensure that the barrels are out of the way of the loading chutes for the coal bunkers. There is photographic evidence available on the web for this practice. Having the guns in their normal positions would have got in the way of the booms and tackles used to get the coal sacks from one ship to the other. At this stage I was about halfway through the construction of the ship

▶ This is a slightly closer view. It is not a kit for a beginner or the faint-hearted. Note the structure between the funnels, for carrying the ship's boats. This was cast in resin, and needed extremely careful sanding to detach it from the casting film. This is a part that would have been better made from photo-etch. The bridge wing, with the circular platform attached was cast with solid bulwarks, as was the deck below. When I cut the bulwarks off, the rest of the part was too delicate and shattered. I needed to replace it with a piece cut from plasticard. I have put some crew figures on the superstructure. They are operating the coaling winches. I put them in place at this early stage because I would not have been able to get access later. A bit of forethought is always useful. The circular objects on the deck are the loading chutes or scuttles for the

coal bunkers. I have drilled out the more forward ones, to show them as open. Regarding the painting, filters in various colours of extremely dilute oil paint have been randomly applied over the grey paint to break up the appearance a bit. Apart from drybrushing with a very light grey, weathering has been kept to an absolute minimum. This is a peacetime scene, and the ship would have been kept totally spick and span. That being said, I will be applying a LOT of grime to the deck later on!

The diorama represents my interpretation of one method of carrying this out; transferring coal from a collier and from lighters. I used the Combrig 1/700 kit of HMS *Indomitable*. This was a very convenient choice for me, as the original builder's model of the ship is displayed in the Riverside Museum in Glasgow, close to where I live. The merchant ship is from the kit of ss *Drumgeith*, by Battlefleet Models. In addition, lighters and a tugboat were obtained from Fine Waterline

▲ This is the collier. Although the kit is of the ss *Drumgeith*, it is not being used to represent this ship, but really just as a generic merchant ship. The coal trade was one of the largest branches of shipping around the British coast in the nineteenth and early twentieth centuries. The coal ship would have been the equivalent of the petrol tanker on our modern roads. The Battlefleet Models kit is a relatively simple one and can benefit from a bit of improvement in detail. If I remember correctly, I thinned down the bulwarks to the main deck and added some inboard detail, replaced the ventilators with resin copies of those from a Combrig HMS *Royal Sovereign* and used lifeboats from the spares box. The masts, derricks and boat davits were from brass rod and wire. In contrast to the battlecruiser, the paintwork on this ship is mucky, heavily streaked and grimed. It isn't a pretty ship, but it has personality. It is just like the one in John Masefield's poem Cargoes:

'Dirty British coaster with salt-caked smoke stack,
Butting through the Channel in the mad March days'

▲ Looking down on the collier, you can see what else I have done. I hollowed out the holds with a Dremel-type tool and a coarse cutter. I went right through the bottom of the hull casting, and also undercut on all sides to give the impression of the hold extending out to the sides of the ship. The hatch coamings were damaged and replaced with plastic strip. The openings under the hull were sealed with pieces of paper. These 'floors' to the holds were then covered on the inside with PVA glue and sprinkled with fine sand. When painted black it looked like a cargo of loose coal. You can also see crew figures in the holds, busily shovelling coal into sacks, which are then attached to the derrick tackles

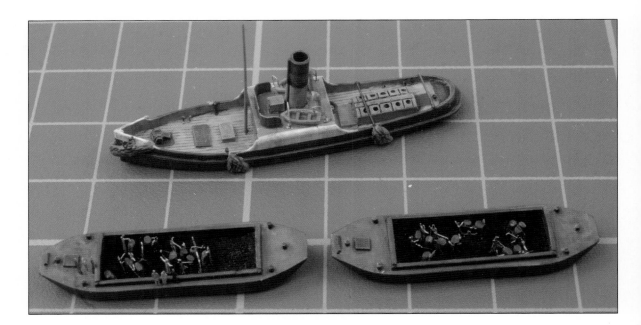

▲ These are the Thames lighters and a little tugboat from the turn of the nineteenth to twentieth centuries. They were produced by Fine Waterline and are probably no longer available. They are extremely short-run semi-kits, consisting of little more than a basic hull casting for the modeller to build upon. They are produced by amateur modellers on a non-commercial basis, with profits going to charity. I produced some Thames sailing barges for them, and I can assure you that these, at least, were true kitchen table castings! Again, you can notice the crew figures in the lighters, and the coal represented by painted sand. The brown cylinders are the sacks, and made from Milliput, rolled into a long string and cut off into short pieces

◄ This photo and the next one illustrate my thought processes in planning the layout of the diorama. At this stage I knew what vessels would be in it, and the size of the base. The precise positioning of the various elements was not so certain. The collier would be on one side of the ship and the lighters on the other. I had always intended that the lighters would be alongside the forward superstructure. The coal chutes in the battlecruiser's deck had already been drilled out to reflect this arrangement. To give a balanced composition, the tugboat needed to be on the same side as the lighters. Note a few important points here. As usual, the ships are not parallel to the sides of the base, but neither are they on the full diagonal. The larger triangles in the opposite corners give space for activity to be shown; in this case, the tugboat. I have positioned the battlecruiser so that there is slightly more space on its starboard side, so that the collier is not cramped. But with this orientation, the tugboat is forced to be at the same end as the lighters, and this makes it feel a bit unbalanced. So this was not the arrangement that I finally decided upon

◀ Here I have moved things around towards the opposite diagonal. The effect of this is to give a larger area beside the battlecruiser's stern on the port side. The tugboat is now at the opposite end of the diorama to the lighters and is spaced more satisfactorily. It is also a bit more obvious how I have positioned the battlecruiser very slightly towards the rear of the base, the right hand side in this photo. As the collier is much bigger than the lighters, it needs a bit more space to look right. However, there is a resulting large area of empty water in the bottom left corner, a bit too big. I am going to put a small sailing boat down here. This is going to give some interest that would otherwise be lacking. It is also going to be pointing in the opposite direction to the other vessels, and provide a visual counterbalance and help to draw the eye back into the main action

▶ Here we can see a couple of frets of photo-etched figures. The upper one is by Flyhawk and the lower one by Lion Roar. As I said earlier, they have a large variety of poses, that are not too stereotyped or ludicrous. Admittedly, the Flyhawk fret does have a lot of men saluting and a fair few others with arms outstretched, but then it has some that are kneeling or bending, and useful for a diorama of men working. The bottom four rows on the Lion Roar fret are figures that are intended to be bent into whatever pose you wish. This will help to get over the two-dimensional appearance that is the main problem with photo-etched figures. I have painted the fret to represent different forms of clothing, ratings in white working dress, brown overalls, and blue for officers and petty officers. You can also see the coal sacks made from Milliput, rolled out and cut into short pieces

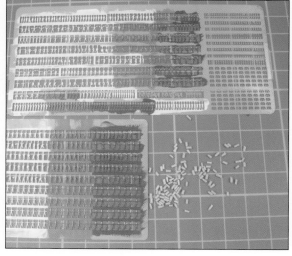

◀ Here I have rubbed powdered graphite from pencil lead over both sides of the fret, to represent the filth that covered everything. I have never understood why white has been a traditional colour for sailors' uniforms. Particularly as a working dress, it must be virtually impossible to keep clean and smart on a crowded ship with minimal washing facilities. Photos of sailors involved in coaling appear to show that some are wearing civilian clothes, and maybe that was a way of getting around the problem

▲ The battlecruiser is seen mounted in its final position on the base. I wanted to complete everything on this ship before I mounted the other vessels. I would have found it impossible to do the rigging, or fix photo-etched railings if the collier was in the way. Note the cage aerials for wireless telegraphy. This is a very complex bit of rigging, and a few years ago I worked out a way of doing it that has a convincing scale appearance. The process is shown in detail in my previous book. Also notice the line that appears to be running between the funnels. In fact, it is on the far side, and is rigged to support the tackles that are being used to hoist the sacks of coal from the lighters. The collier, which will be on this side of *Indomitable*, will be using its own derricks for this purpose

◀ These are crew figures shifting coal sacks around and tipping the contents into the bunkers. I have not used an enormous number of figures. In real life most of the ship's company would be involved. But if had used many more figures, I reckon they would have been too crowded. Towards the left of the picture is the ship's band, with blue drums, and a man with a camera on a tripod is taking their photograph

This and the following photos show the completed diorama. I am very pleased with the way it has turned out. Unfortunately, at the time of writing, it, along with three other ships, has suffered severe damage at the hands (or paws) of one of my cats, and it will have to undergo a few weekends of repair work. I assure you that the cat did NOT receive severe damage in return at my own hands, though it was a close thing! For a few minutes it was a matter of 'Doodle, be afraid. Be very afraid!'

CHAPTER 4

SAFELY IN HARBOUR

A scene with one or more ships tied up at a quayside is a perennially popular subject for a diorama. And there is good reason why this should be so. There is an immediate relationship between the ship and the dockside, and any activity taking place there. If there is more than one vessel, then the dock gives them a reason to be close together. Whether they are moored beside or in front of one another, those mooring cables that cross over each other pull them together into a unified arrangement.

The dock itself gives the modeller an open space to fill with all manner of paraphernalia: machinery, cranes, vehicles, trains, various types of goods and stores. And lots of people, both seamen and dock workers.

It is possible to show all sorts of different themes: loading or unloading merchant ships, taking on stores or ammunition for warships, repairing, refitting, repainting, coming home and welcoming, casting off and saying farewell. In that one sentence alone, I have given myself inspiration for enough projects to last me four years.

Harbour buildings are as varied as the ships that get moored next to them. There is scope for a lot of scratch-building and even more use of the imagination. Even if you do not live in a port, you can get inspiration and detail from industrial buildings old and new.

There are harbours large, small and tiny. At one extreme you have US Navy yards, with piers that cover acres and acres. On the other hand you could do something involving a small European port, with tramp steamers or coasters. At the bottom end of the scale, what about a colourful British narrow boat, unloading coal or taking on a cargo of iron or pottery from a factory situated just beside the canal.

It doesn't even need to be a harbour. With me mentioning narrow boats, an idea just flashed through my mind! A canal in Yorkshire, at the entrance to the Standedge Tunnel, dug under the Pennines. A narrow boat is coming out of the tunnel, boatmen lying on boards, having 'legged' the boat through the darkness for three miles. Another narrow boat is waiting its turn to go through, while the horse is led up the path and over

the hill, to re-join the boat on the other side. There you go. If you want to use that suggestion, go ahead. It isn't copyrighted. Just mention where you got the idea, and I'll be happy!

PLANNING

If you have decided to make a harbour diorama, I suspect that you started off with a particular ship kit in mind. Maybe it's going to be one major vessel, but maybe more than one. Or perhaps you have some harbour craft, tugs or lighters that you want to use.

One of the next most important things to consider is the overall size of the arrangement. If you are having a single ship against the dock, then it may not be too much of a problem, even if you are working in 1/350 scale. Two ships moored side by side may also be quite acceptable and can give a base that is neatly proportioned, not too long for its width.

But what if you are going to have two ships moored one in front of the other. A very logical arrangement, certainly, but it will be a very long narrow base that won't look satisfying. So, what to do about it? Perhaps make the base wider, and have more water in front of the ships. But that gives an expanse of empty space that needs something in it. No problem; have a tugboat chugging past. If you don't fancy that idea, then what about making the dock a pier, and having the two ships in line on one side and a third ship on the other, with sheds down the middle of the pier. That would give a well-proportioned base. Or there's the possibility of two piers, with different buildings and equipment, the basin between with the ships and the piers joined at the landward end by the main quay.

Do you see where I'm going with this? The more you want to do, the larger the project becomes. Before starting off down this road, think very carefully, and ask yourself some important questions. Do you have enough time in the year, or in your life to finish it? Will you get bored? Is there enough money in the piggy bank? Is there enough space in the house to keep it once it's done? Do you really want to store it in a cold garage or push it under the spare bed? Is your wife sympathetic to the idea? How much do divorce lawyers cost, and do they take plastic? (And I'm talking Visa, not polystyrene!)

I'm not trying to suggest that it is always a bad idea to plan something big, but it is necessary to have your eye on the big picture, the final planned outcome. And do bear in mind that small can be beautiful too.

So let's now consider what is available on the market to facilitate building your harbour. I suppose that it's sensible to think about the piers and quays themselves, as that is what everything else, ships and boats apart, is going to sit on. These will take one of a number of forms, depending on size, function, or location in the world. Some will be wood, some stone, some brick, some concrete.

Some will have wooden pilings around the outside, some steel.

Resin quays and piers are available from a couple of after-market companies, but from what I have seen of them, I am not greatly impressed. Pilings tend to be uneven, and voids in the moulds cause a lot of excess resin that needs to be trimmed away. I reckon that it's easy to do better by scratch-building your own. The commercially available quays appear to be based on prototypes from US Navy yards, which is not terribly helpful for other subjects.

I shall show you various approaches to quays and piers later in this chapter, and in other 'how to' sections of the book.

In contrast to model railway enthusiasts, small scale ship modellers are rather short on choice when it comes to commercially produced kits of buildings. For instance, plastic kits for hangars, warehouses and barrack blocks are available from Skywave. I have never seen inside the boxes, so I cannot comment on their quality or the age of the mouldings. A number of 1/700 buildings used to be made by Loose Cannon. From the pictures on their website, these appeared as though they could be very useful, but they seem to have stopped producing them. A firm called Goffy used to make

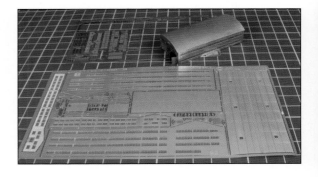

▲ Something a bit more complicated. These are a couple of photo-etched sets from Alliance Model Works. I tried putting the warehouse with the curved roof together to see how it fitted, and found it really very simple. It required some pieces of plastic strip along some of the inside edges so that there was sufficient surface area for glue to attach. The style of building is very much that of a US Navy base. But Alliance is an American company with the same customer base, so I am not making a criticism here! On the contrary, these have the Griffith Seal of Approval!

▼ This is the set of dockside buildings produced by Battlefleet Models. They are simple, well moulded, and the smaller ones are very generic and usable anywhere. The largest building appears to correlate well with photos of those in, I believe, New York Navy Yard. But I have seen these mouldings being used to represent buildings in other parts of the world, and if you, as the modeller, do not mind, then you ought not to feel obliged to lose sleep over it

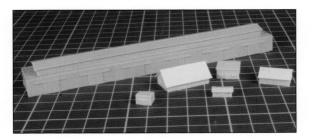

1/350 buildings of a rather generic character, but they have now gone out of business.

So what do we have? Let me show you some of the things that are currently around on the market, and give you some ideas of my own.

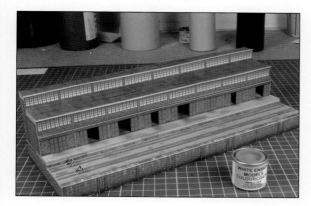

▲ This is a paper model of a harbour building by Hamburger Modellbaubogen Verlag of Hamburg. Paper models are popular in Europe and a vast variety of subjects is available. The standard ship scale is 1/200. You may be tempted to scan the sheets into your computer and print out at a different scale. Be aware that this will breach copyright. It is necessary to get consent from the publishers first. At the very least they will expect you to have purchased the original model, and keep it on your bookshelves when you have finished with it. Any copy you make must under no circumstances be offered for sale, and should not even be given away. 'You have been warned!'

▶ Here we can see one of the drawbacks of photographing buildings. I had a solid fence right at my back, so in order to get the roofline into the shot, I had to angle the camera upwards. This is despite me winding the tripod up so high that I could hardly see through the viewfinder! You can see the phenomenon of converging verticals. The human brain compensates for what the eye tells it, but the camera is not so clever. You can get around this by printing out the photograph, and doing a bit of simple geometry, using the ground line as a datum. Alternatively, Photoshop it, if you are a geek! In addition, the vertical distances are going to be a bit foreshortened towards the top of the image, so measurements are going to be only estimates. If you turn to my final chapter, 'The Silver Darlings', I make buildings from plasticard, using photos as references

▼ If you want to do something a bit less mainstream, especially when it is of a civilian nature, you may feel it necessary to scratch-build your own buildings. Using simple equipment, you can make buildings that, while not entirely accurate, are inspired by those that you can find around you. This is one of a series of photos that I took of the Meiklejohn Building in Glasgow, which used to belong to the John Brown Shipyard, but is now leased out as a boxing gym. A measuring tape will give you the length and depth of the ground plan. The sighting sticks that I have placed against the wall are 2.1 metres long, so that each blue and white section is 700mm long. This will then equate to 1mm in 1/700 scale or 2mm in 1/350. You can thus estimate heights of walls and sizes of windows, etc

▶ A set of Mississippi barges from Battlefleet Models. You almost have a ready-made diorama here, complete in one box. And there is one of those ubiquitous little tugboats again. You just can't get away from them nowadays!

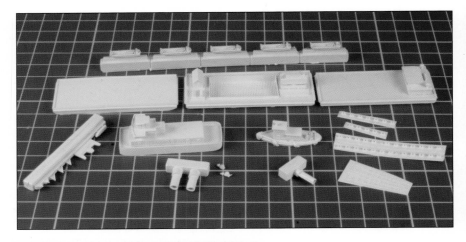

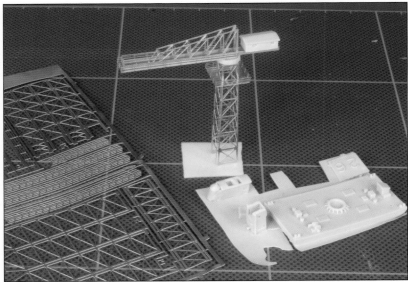

◀ Dockyards and harbours have cranes. If you are looking for something that is adding background interest, then there is a lot to be said for the straightforward Loose Cannon products. There are companies that make cranes with much more detail and finesse, and enormously more complicated. You may want that if the crane is the centre of attention, but otherwise these do the job nicely. The brass is relatively thick and bends easily and forgivingly. Even a beginner in brass can make something quite presentable

▶ White Ensign and L'Arsenal both make 1/700 vehicles and railway rolling stock in resin. But I thought these looked rather fun! Photo-etched brass from Alliance Model Works, once again. It all looks rather daunting on the fret, but the parts cut away readily and the folds are also easy to make. This fret contains enough parts for two diesel-electric switchers and fourteen assorted waggons, along with some track, telegraph poles and trackside signals

◀ OK, from the sublime to the ridiculous. These vehicles are 1/700 scale. That is my own thumb; it does not belong to my giant cousin! They are by a new company called Five Star. Believe it or not, and you'd better believe it, that deuce-and-a-half truck consists of twenty eight individual parts, and could have had thirty three if I'd put the tilt hoops in! Each rear wheel has four parts. The whole set has enough parts for fourteen trucks, with a variety of bodies, and nine jeeps, with some trailers. I had to put these together, because if I'd only photographed the fret, you'd never have thought they were actually do-able. And now I think I hear that nice nurse coming down the corridor with my afternoon medication. I hope she'll loosen the straps on my straight-jacket, it's chafing me a bit!

▶ And now for a few examples of harbour dioramas by some of my colleagues. This is one by Jim Baumann. It uses as its main subject the 1/700 resin kit of a Hog Islander freighter, made by Battlefleet Models. It is a real *tour-de-force* in terms of demonstrating modelling skills. But as a diorama it has a couple of weaknesses, and Jim agrees about them. Firstly, you will notice that everything is parallel to the sides of the base, and this weakens the artistic arrangement of the diorama. Secondly, it is very crowded, and this makes it difficult to notice the main points of interest. There are too many of them. Jim says that he kept getting more bits and pieces sent from Battlefleet, and felt obliged to include them all, so it kept getting more and more filled up! (PHOTO BY JIM BAUMANN)

▶ This diorama by Peter Fulgoney has a similar theme. It uses the same Hog Islander and harbour craft as Jim's. But I think it works better. The freighter is not parallel to the quay, and the tugs have an obvious relationship to it. There is a movement that the previous diorama lacks. And the inclusion of a bit of empty water allows the eye to roam around more. (PHOTO BY PETER FULGONEY)

▲ Mike McCabe was inspired by some photos of the port of Gdynia in Poland to make a diorama depicting the Polish fleet, just before the outbreak of the Second World War. Niko produce almost the whole Polish navy in 1/700, so choice of subjects is easy. Mike has not attempted to replicate Gdynia docks exactly, which must look totally different today, but has attempted to give an impression of what they were like. Although the vessels are moored parallel to each other and to the quayside, Mike has managed to arrange it so that the whole composition is slightly off square, in the way that I like. He is also unafraid to leave some empty spaces here and there. (PHOTO BY MIKE MCCABE)

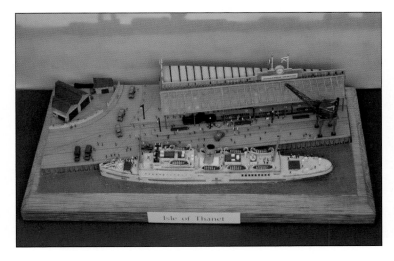

Isle of Thanet

◀ Another of Mike's dioramas shows the hospital ship *Isle of Thanet* pulling into Dunkirk at the start of the evacuation of the BEF in 1940. Notice how the buildings have been cut off at angles where they extend outside the 'frame'. The convoy of ambulances tells the story. There is also some movement from the ship. My only quibble with it is that I would have preferred to see the figures grouped a bit more, rather than evenly spread. But even so, I regard it as a most attractive and effective diorama. (Photo by Mike McCabe)

'RETURN OF THE BUCCANEERS'

My harbour diorama is really quite a simple one, compared to the work of some of my friends that I am showcasing in this chapter. But it demonstrates a few points that I'd like to make.

Browsing around my local hobby shop one day, I noticed the 1/700 scale submarines made by Hobby Boss. They were extremely simple kits, with only about six or so parts above the waterline, but quite nicely detailed, at least in regards to the main parts. And at only about four quid each, you could hardly go wrong. They yelled at me, 'Buy several of us. Moor us at a dockside!' Decision made, simple!

More solid inspiration came from photos of submarines and dockyard craft found on Navsource. Here I found a lot of detail about what the docksides looked like and how the workshop barges would be moored relative to the submarines. Also the sort of clutter that would be found on the quay.

I bought four submarine kits, two Gato Class and two Balao. I wanted to demonstrate the variety of armament fits that the boats carried, as well as the different camouflage measures used. I was not trying to represent any particular submarines, just generic boats, as they would have looked towards the end of the war. One has been given a name, USS *Anchovy*, and that is totally fictional. I didn't want some rivet counter saying something along the lines of, 'The USS *Stickleback* never had that number of 40mm guns, wore a different colour scheme, and by the way, she was sunk in 1943!'

I wanted to depict a submarine returning to its main base for a refit, after a protracted time away across the other side of the Pacific. There will be a welcoming party on the quayside, colleagues, wives, girlfriends, nurses, maybe even a few ladies of easy virtue.

This was another occasion where I used the scratch-built dockyard barges that I showed you when I was building the *Langley*. In fact, I think that I originally built them for this diorama. Not that it really matters.

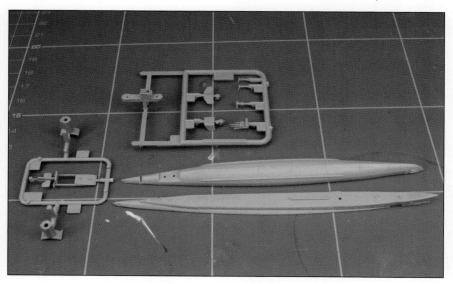

These are all the parts for one submarine. I think this one is a Gato, by the rather more slender periscope housings. As you can see, there are a mere seven parts required for a waterline model. The guns are a bit crudely moulded, and need some replacements. The smaller guns are only 20mm ones, and by 1945, at least one 40mm would have been mounted. Luckily, some rather nice resin parts are available

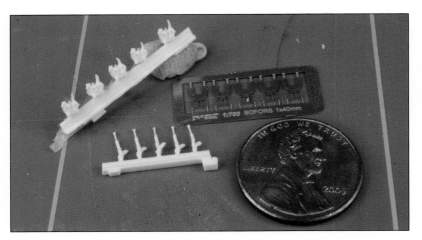

◀ The Polish company Niko makes some delightful replacement parts for 1/700 scale, updating the over-scale injected moulded components with much more lifelike offerings. In particular they have anti-aircraft and destroyer gun mountings for the major WWII navies, as well as lorries, cargo boxes and Japanese landing craft. Here you can see 40mm single mounts. Each submarine will mount at least one of these

▶ I had bought a length of resin dockside from one of the after-market companies, but was not terribly satisfied with it, and thought I could do better myself. This is what I did. I took a core of balsa wood. Using two-part epoxy, I glued Evergreen strip around both edges and the end, and plasticard over the top. The wooden piles and rubbing strake were added from some more thin Evergreen strip. The surface of the plasticard was too smooth, even at this scale, to be convincing for concrete, so I softened it by brushing liquid cement over it, and then gently tapped it, in a random pattern, with coarse sandpaper. This broke the starkness up ever so slightly. When everything had solidified again, I scribed parallel lines to represent railway tracks. These would become more obvious later on after a wash of oil paint picked them out

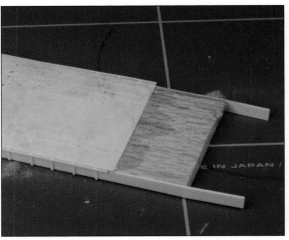

◀ This is a little tugboat from Battlefleet Models. It comes in a set with a larger type. The level of detail is moderately good, although since this photo was taken an improved version has been released with photo-etched shim to cover the superstructure. The tugboat will eventually be moored at the end of the pier, simply to provide another focus of interest and a sense of scale for comparison against the submarines. The white object is a barge from another Battlefleet set. I decided that this was an unsuitable size and shape for this diorama, and did not use it

▶ I chose one of the smallest cranes on the Loose Cannon fret. After all, this is one of the piers in the submarine base. It is not the place where battleships are fitted out, so I hardly wanted to overpower everything else by using a gigantic hammerhead or Titan crane. The brass folded very easily. The visible gaps along the corner uprights of the tower can be filled up with diluted PVA glue prior to painting

▼ This is one of the submarines midway through the construction process. There isn't really a lot to say, except that it shows that I try to make things easy for myself by painting major structures before adding smaller details, railings, etc. I have applied a couple of washes of dilute oils over the basic paint, but it needs some touching up and straightening out here and there. It will also get some drybrushing

◀ The tugboat at a similar stage. The grooves and shadows could do with a bit more emphasis by way of increasing the amount of pin-wash. It also needs a bit more streaking of rust and grime. And those bollards look far too long. They need trimming down before the model is finished

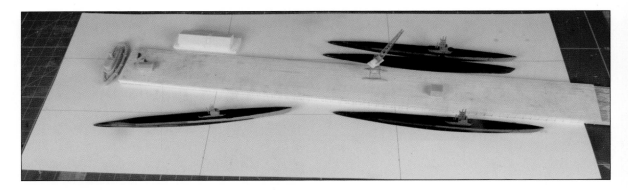

▲ This is a preliminary stage in my working out of the arrangement of the diorama. I eventually came up with something a bit different, and hopefully more interesting, as well. Following my usual practice, the pier is on an angle. I have marked lines on the paper, dividing it into thirds, each way. I have tried, but not too hard, to position the main foci of interest close to the intersections of these lines. Artists call this the 'Rule of Thirds'. You can see this best at the conning tower of the boat at the left. After some consideration, I decided that there was too much weight towards the right, and I moved the two boats on the far side about two inches to the left. This gave space for another barge at the far right. I also put a barge in the foreground, beside the right hand submarine, to balance the scene more

▼ The base is ready to start receiving the vessels. A sheet of watercolour paper covers the base. It has been painted a deep bluish grey, to represent Pacific waters. The paint is fairly even, as the surface will be calm. It has not yet had a coat of acrylic gel. The pier is painted a mottled concrete colour, with greenish brown down the sides for wood covered in seaweed

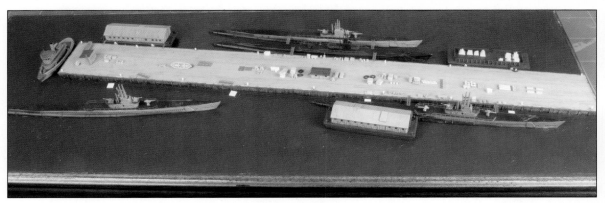

▲ The vessels have been glued in position. I put a preliminary coat of acrylic gel on the water surface first, but tried to keep it as thin and smooth as possible. I normally put the gel down after the vessel is fixed, and use it to hide the gaps at the waterline. But it would be very awkward to get it between the vessels and the quay, so the order is reversed. I'll put a second coat on later to the areas that I can reach. I

have started to arrange junk and paraphernalia on the quay. Some of this will be packing cases from Evergreen strip, but a lot consists of small parts left over from old kits and recovered from the spares box. I do not intend these to be recognised as what they were originally supposed to be, but just to give the impression of piles of 'Stuff, assorted, naval dockyards for the use of'

◀ A close up of two of the submarines. Although the railings had a coat of primer before being cut from the fret, they will get a more definitive painting during the final touching up stage. Deck extensions around the deck guns are formed by a film of PVA glue. The reflection of this can be seen at top right. The deck guns came from the spares box. You can just make out one of a different pattern on the black submarine

▶ This is some of the assorted junk. The bits cut from sprues out of other kits are not supposed to actually 'be' what the mouldings suppose them to be, but just to give the impression of the piles of equipment, stores and spare parts that would be accumulated in a dockyard. I can recognise some bits of 40mm gun barrels and some gun directors, but can't say where the other bits come from. It betrays my age when I say that it reminds me of the cover from Steeleye Span's album *Commoner's Crown*, which has a crown made from lots of little Airfix figures, glued together and painted gold. I spent hours of my wasted youth trying to work out which sets they had bought to make it; Guards Colour Party, British Paratroopers, etc!

◀ This barge contains some palleted loads from Battlefleet Models. The fenders are made from epoxy putty, but I could equally well have used photo-etched lifebuoy rings to represent car tyres. The railway tracks are just engraved into the surface of the quay. The two in the middle are supposed to be standard gauge, while the outer ones fit the wheels of the crane

▶ The gangways passing between the dockside and the subs are just lengths of photo-etched inclined ladder, albeit not actually inclining. The mooring lines are copper wire. I had tried to colour this with a horribly toxic potion called Blacken-It, but the coating came off easily and I will have to touch it up with a fine paintbrush later on

▼ What do we have here? Piles of squares of grooved plasticard for empty pallets. A little generator-type thingy on four wheels. Barrels or oil drums made from plastic rod. I'm rather pleased with the general appearance of trolleys for oxy-acetylene cylinders, even though they are rather too big. Note the way that I have painted the pilings and sides of the dock in browny-green colours to represent a mixture of grime, oil and seaweed

▼ There now follow a few photos of the completed diorama. I'll let them speak for themselves

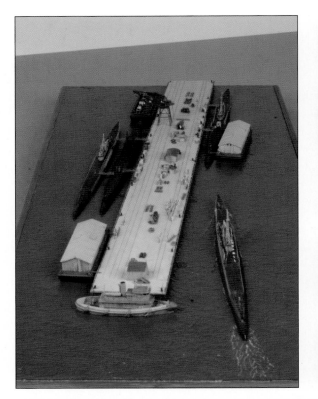

DON McKEAND'S LONDONDERRY DIORAMA

I was very impressed with Don McKeand's diorama of the River Foyle in Londonderry (or Derry, depending on your heritage or point of view) in 1942, when I saw it at Telford. He was kind enough to send me a set of photographs of not only the completed diorama, but also the design and construction process, a few of which I am delighted to show here. Unfortunately I have not been able to include photos of individual ships as they were being built, due to small file sizes being unsuitable for publication.

Don has told me that he has been fascinated by the Battle of the Atlantic for many years, ever since seeing HMS *Pelican* being broken up on his journeys to school. He had been planning this kind of diorama for quite a time and got the final push from seeing the Liverpool Docks diorama, built as a joint effort by the 'German Gamblers', which appears later on in the book.

This is an overall view of the diorama. The size is 47cm by 31cm. The shape of the river is impressionistic rather than strictly accurate, as aerial photos from Google Earth show that it is not as sharply curved as is shown here. But this arrangement gives a better artistic feel to the diorama and makes it less linear. The eyes move around it better and find it more satisfying than they might otherwise. Don admits that his sources for the buildings were scanty, but he is fairly confident that the relative positions of the main structures are roughly correct for this stretch of the river. If you have access to such things as large scale Ordnance Survey maps from the time in question, then you can be certain of the layout of roads and the sizes and 'footprints' of buildings on the ground. For contemporary information, images from Google Earth can be useful. It is surprising to find that high security facilities like naval dockyards are not blanked out, even in countries such as Russia. Even North Korea isn't represented by a void between South Korea and China!

He wanted to show Londonderry at the height of the battle, and to demonstrate the activity in the city, the variety and numbers of vessels in the River Foyle, their different configurations and camouflage schemes and the crowded way they were moored along the river.

His sources included photographs from a booklet entitled *Atlantic Memorial*, produced by the harbour museum at Londonderry, and which gave a good impression of the atmosphere and information about the buildings. He got photos of the ships that he wanted to include from the Imperial War Museum, amongst other sources.

The ship models came from a variety of sources. Flower Class corvettes were modified from White Ensign resin kits. HMS *Leith* was from a 'craftsman' type kit of a Grimsby Class sloop from Fine Waterline. HMS *Egret*, another sloop, was scratchbuilt, taking information from photographs, and extrapolating and interpolating from known features of other similar classes of ships. Detail parts were scavenged from other kits, such as a Tamiya E class destroyer.

The store carrier *Robert Dundas* was also scratch-built from photographic references. Don tells me that he used the 'egg box' method of construction using plasticard. The waterline shape is cut out first, and then a longitudinal spine and transverse formers are cut to shape and glued to it. The deck goes on top next, and finally the hull is skinned with rather thinner plasticard. This is quite a simple method of construction, suitable for ships that have fairly straight-sided hulls. It would not be possible to use it for hulls that have complex curves or very rounded sterns, such as the corvettes.

The diorama is not intended to show an exact scene on a particular day, but more to be representative of the ships that served in the various escort groups that were based in the city in 1942. (PHOTOS COURTESY OF DON McKEAND.)

▶ From the few available photos, which gave him most of the information, Don drew plans to 1/700 scale of the buildings that he wanted to use. In addition to those in the book, he also obtained some old postcards of Londonderry in the first half of the twentieth century, which gave inspiration as to the appearance of the types of buildings to be seen there. Imagination played a part, however. Bryce's factory, the grey building with skylights in the roof, which can be seen in the first photo, was largely conjectural.

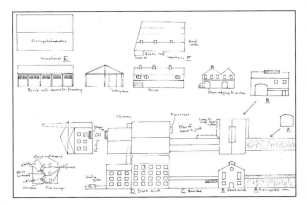

▲ The buildings have been made from plasticard. Where possible, and where size permitted, the windows were cut out and backed with bits of photo-etched railings to make the glazing bars. I don't know whether the buildings have been glued to the base at this stage. I suspect not, as it would be much easier to paint them if they were not attached. To some extent the buildings are following their positions on the ground in real life, but in the absence of really definitive data, Don did not feel too constrained and was happy to use a little bit of imagination, in order to arrive at something that 'felt' right. Notice the sheet of watercolour paper that will form the water surface. When you are gluing such a large piece of paper, the forces of contraction exerted as the glue dries can cause the baseboard to distort. For this reason, it is good practice to glue another sheet of paper to the underside to counteract the bending. 'Been there, done that, got the tee-shirt!'

▲ This photo shows some of the ships in the completed diorama. At the extreme left the tug *Jaunty* is backing up towards the *Robert Dundas*, churning the mud as she does so. Next are the destroyers *Fame* and *Whitehall*, converted from Tamiya kits of an E Class destroyer and HMAS

Vampire. Then the sloops *Leith*, *Rochester* and *Egret*. At the extreme right are partial views of the four Flowers. If you look closely, you can see just how different they all are, even though they are sister ships. The odd shaped craft at the front is the boom defence vessel *Barcross*, again scratch-built.

◀ This is a rather evocative photo of the whole thing. The low angle of the sun makes it look almost as though it is sunset on a summer night. It illustrates the way these ships were moored very close to each other. If it weren't for the appearance of dropping off the edge of the World just a few yards astern of the corvettes, this would be a very realistic picture. Never mind

◀ This factory building shows how Don used photo-etched ships' railing for the glazing bars in the rather larger windows. And look at the light traffic on the road, compared to nowadays. In 1942 few people had cars, and those that did, had petrol rationing to put up with. For readers outside these little islands, note that we drive on the left!

▲ Another charming and atmospheric photo. It looks as though the sun has now almost dropped below the horizon. But as the River Foyle runs roughly north-south, the shadows indicate that the sun is not in the west. But, hey, what the hell? It's a nice photo!

CHAPTER 5

'ALL ON ITS OWNSOME'

This is about having a ship on its own, without any supporting craft or vessels, in the sea, and calling it a diorama. Now I know that some people will turn round and say to me, 'It can't be a diorama. You've got to have more than one thing to call it a diorama.'

This is a point of view that springs from the strict definitions that competitions have, written to decide how models should be apportioned to the various classes, and make the judging fair. These rules may be necessary, but I don't think they ought to dictate how we use our imaginations in designing our models. Personally, I don't care two hoots about the rules of any competition. I make models to satisfy myself. If I have to put the model into one class and not another, so be it. I don't really enter competitions to win prizes, although I do take the hump if the judging has been very unfair. I put the models on the competition tables because people look more closely at them than if they were on the club table.

So if you wish to take the view that a single ship cannot be a diorama I will not argue with you too much. But that is not really what this book is about. It is about putting an element of 'life' into your models, and it is every bit as valid to do this to an isolated single ship as it is to do it to a group of them.

Maybe you sincerely believe that a single ship cannot be called a 'diorama', whatever the circumstances. But let me try to persuade you otherwise. If you go back to the first chapter, you will find that I list some ideas, subjects and themes that can be incorporated into dioramas. Some of them can be equally applicable to a composition that incorporates only one vessel, as they are to those that have more than one, or other elements.

You may choose to show some activity happening on board a ship. A number of things spring to mind: the crew lined up on parade, or perhaps manning the deck edges as the ship is dressed overall with flags for the Fleet Review. There could be more mundane activity such as swabbing the decks, sailors lining up to collect their pay, or playing sports, such as a boxing match or tug o' war. A photo in a book that I have about the Victorian navy shows crew members going through the exercises of cutlass drill on the quarterdeck. I've always thought that it would make a rather fascinating arrangement, and the 1/700 figures from Lion Roar, that can be bent to take whatever pose you like, would make it entirely possible.

Or drama on board a ship. What about the crew fighting desperately to contain the damage from the effects of gunfire, bombing or a *kamikaze* hit? Or the other side of the equation, the combat situations that I previously spoke about. Or a ship may be sinking. At Telford in 2012 the diorama that took the bronze medal had only one quarter of a ship, the stern of the *Titanic*, just about to disappear below the waves.

Or an emotional scene. How about the crew of a damaged warship, paraded on deck dressed in their whites, with the bodies of dead comrades covered by flags and about to be consigned to the deep by the captain or padre?

All of these subjects could be considered as worthy subjects for dioramas, even if some of them could just as well be entered into single ship classes in competitions. If I were being cynical, then I could suggest waiting for a while before choosing which class to enter until you have sized up the opposition. But I know you'd NEVER be so sneaky or conniving, would you?

So, let's look at a few models that involve only one ship.

▲ This is my model of the light carrier USS *San Jacinto*. When I bought the kit, labelled as 'Premium Edition' by Dragon, I expected something quite special. I was quite disappointed when I examined it more closely and found that the basic mouldings were twenty-year-old Pit Road ones, with the addition of a small fret of photo-etch and a totally gimmicky transparent flight deck, which would reveal that the hangar deck was moulded some six feet too low. Construction was something of a struggle. I have never called the completed model a diorama, but I could do if I wanted. I include it to show that the addition of figures and activity to a model brings life and interest

▼ The deck of the *San Jacinto*. The crew are moving the aircraft to the stern, in preparation for an airstrike. The varied poses that Lion Roar include on their fret come in very useful here. This is even one of those occasions where I am glad of all those little men with both arms upraised, because they are ideal for pushing against the wing of an aircraft! But close-up photography is a harsh critic. Look at those Oerlikon tubs. I really should have tried harder to eliminate those sloping verticals that Dragon's earlier kits are notorious for

I chose to open up the lift and the roller shutters in the sides of the ship, and then include some rudimentary details inside the hangar. The deck has been raised to the (approximately) correct level and some framing added to the insides of the bulkheads in areas that are visible. I also scratch-built the 40mm guns to replace the awful things included in the kit. I found that the photo-etched guns from White Ensign were over-scale, and this model was built before the resin offerings from Niko had started to become available

This is the Czarist Russian battleship *Potemkin*, depicted during the famous mutiny in 1905. Why anyone would want to show her at any other time is beyond me! The story goes that the ship sailed past the rest of the Black Sea Fleet, with their guns trained upon her. Her crew were cheering and trying to persuade the crews of the other ships to mutiny as well, but feared all the time that they would be fired upon. If I were doing this model again, I think I would include more figures on the deck. Note also the colours of the funnels. Although the official colour scheme called for them to be an ochre colour, a photo taken during the mutiny shows unequivocally that *Potemkin*'s were white.

▲ Jim Baumann's model of HMS *Furious* shows what I mean by having some activity on a ship. The little airship certainly adds a lot of life and interest. I'm not sure what it is made of or how it is supported, but it certainly looks every bit as though it is lighter than air. (PHOTO BY JIM BAUMANN)

▼ A single ship in a dramatic setting. The Austro-Hungarian battleship *Szent Iztván* was torpedoed by the Italians during the First World War. The subdued lighting and cloudy background that Jim has used in his photo adds to the sense of foreboding and tragedy surrounding the doomed ship. (PHOTO BY JIM BAUMANN)

USS ASTORIA

The Combrig 1/700 resin kit of the USS *Astoria* had been sitting in my stash, in a semi-started condition for several years. A couple of photos in Steve Wiper's book on the New Orleans Class cruisers show the *Astoria* in the process of recovering one of her floatplanes, and I used these as inspiration for this diorama

▼ The half-completed model is fixed to the base as the sea surface is being built up. The positioning of the ship away from the centre line is enough to give space for the floatplane off the starboard quarter. It also helps to emphasise that the ship is supposed to be executing a turn to starboard in order to give an area of smooth water for the plane to land on. I have not really managed this very well. Because the ship will be heeling to port as she turns to starboard, I had added a strip of plastic under the waterline to angle the ship away from the vertical. The hatched rectangle in front of the floatplane is the approximate position of the sled that the ship is towing, and onto which the plane will taxi.

And some photos of the completed model. Because the basic conception of the diorama is so simple, there has not been much more to say about its planning and construction. But note one or two things. The sled has been made from a piece cut from a pair of my wife's old nylon tights, and it is being towed on a line rigged on a boom, which is deployed from the foredeck. You can see the other one hanging on the port side of the ship. Steve Wiper's photos seem to show a lot of the crew watching the fun from the starboard side of the quarterdeck, and I have tried to reflect this in the arrangement of the figures

CHAPTER 6

'MAKING HEAVY WEATHER OF IT'

For any ship diorama builder, a vital skill to master is that of making a convincing water surface. Whether it is sea, river or lake, it will feature in all dioramas, except situations like dry docks, or slipways. I dealt with making a basic sea base in my previous book, but as it is so important in the context of a diorama, I have decided to repeat the process here. This is really the only occasion where I am reiterating some area of construction from that book, so I hope you do not feel short-changed. I am also going to demonstrate different approaches to seas, by other expert modellers.

I do not suggest that these are the only methods that you can use. Other modellers may recommend such things as transparent silicone bathroom sealant, crumpled aluminium foil, or building everything up using plaster or wall filling compound. Each modeller will develop his favourite techniques, and if they get good results from them I am not going to say they are wrong. The methods I shall describe are simply the ones that I have found to work well for me, or which I have admired in my friends' work, and would wish to try in the future.

The very first thing to consider is the question of what sort of situation the ship is going to be in, as this will determine to a large extent the best method to use. Is the ship anchored in calm water, moving slowly in a light sea, or pushing against an ocean swell? The materials that you will use will be much the same, but employed in different ways and in different proportions.

MATERIALS

I build any sea surface on a base layer of watercolour paper. Even the thinnest watercolour paper is a lot more robust than most other papers. It comes in a choice of three surface textures, 'Hot Pressed', which is smooth, 'Not', meaning not hot pressed and which is medium texture, and 'Rough', which is obvious. Get the rough finish. It does not need to be the most expensive handmade paper. A medium weight is also the most appropriate for our needs.

If you are making a flat calm, the paper will be glued directly to the wooden baseboard. But if you are aiming to represent an ocean swell some shape or texture will need to be placed under the paper. For this I will use Polyfilla, or any ready mixed filler compound for holes in walls.

The shape of small waves and ripples, as well as the bow waves and wake of the ship will be built up on top of the paper. I find that this is best achieved by using acrylic pastes and gels from the art shop, which come in either opaque or clear forms and in various thicknesses, down to semi-liquid.

I also go to the art shop for paints for the sea. I have tended to use the very cheap brands of acrylic paints that come in squeezy bottles. I have a selection of blues, greens and browns, as well as greys, black and white. If you start off by mixing fairly bright and intense colours, you can arrive at the sort of hue you are looking for and tone it down with grey.

I do not use standard modelling paints for the sea. They tend not to have the bright colours required to get the basic hue, and they are also much more expensive.

Having looked at the work of Werner de Keersmaecker, which I shall show you later on, I am toying with the idea of trying out artist's oil paints for the sea. I don't know if that is what he uses, but I reckon the effects he gets might be most readily achieved with them.

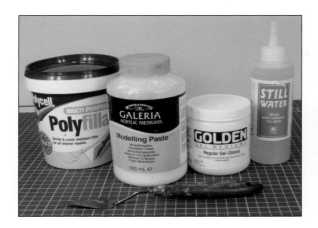

▲ These are the various mixtures that I use. Polyfilla, or a similar 'own brand' wall filler product can be obtained from the hardware store. It sets quickly without a lot of shrinkage. The acrylic paste is used for building up wave forms on top of the paper. It sets quite slowly and with considerable shrinkage, so I would not recommend it for anything that requires a thick layer. Do not try using it to build up the whole of an Atlantic swell. The acrylic gel sets clear and gives a transparent surface to the water with a sense of depth. The stiffer gels can give sharp waves, such as you would see in a ship's bow wave, but the softer ones will enable you to do smooth and gentle ripples. Vallejo Still Water is good for smoothing out excessively sharp ripples on an otherwise calm surface

▲ These are mostly cheapo-cheapo acrylic paints. The colours are bright. You'll never find a sea in those hues of green or blue. But if you mix them up and use enough grey, then you can get just the right colour, whether that is the dark bluish colour of the Pacific, or the paler, greenish grey of the North Sea. Apply them with a brush. Even when diluted, most of these paints will not go through an airbrush well

A BASIC SEA SURFACE

This is the sequence of processes that can be used for a ship moving through a fairly calm sea. The model is that of HMAS *Sydney*, and the photos were previously published in my first book.

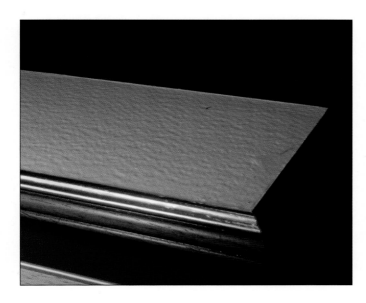

◀ A piece of watercolour paper has been glued on top of the MDF baseboard. The photo has been taken with the light at a low angle to show up the texture of the paper. You can use either PVA glue or a contact adhesive, such as Evo-Stik. I tend to cut the paper over size, and trim the edges when everything is dried out. If you use PVA, the water-based nature of the glue will tend to make the paper shrink slightly as it dries. This may not be a problem with a small 1/700 model, but if you are making a large diorama the considerable forces exerted can cause a significant twist to the base. For this reason, you would be well advised to glue another sheet of paper to the underside of the base to exert a counter-force

▶ I have applied a first layer of acrylic paste to begin building up the shape of the waves. You will note that I have painted the watercolour paper grey. This is simply to allow the white acrylic paste to show up in the photo. It is not something that I would normally do. With this stage I am concentrating on getting the ship's bow wave and wake to look right. The main sea surface is just small random splodges. Try examining photos of real ships to get an idea of the appearance of real bow waves as they move through the water

◀ I have let the first layer dry for 24 hours, and have applied a second coat of acrylic paste to the area outside of the ship's bow wave and wake. I have tried to maintain a sort of visual difference between the two areas, with the wake being shown by a texture that is finer but more agitated. The paste has been applied with a palette knife, but this tool gives a texture that is crude and coarse, so I blended and smoothed the waves with a damp paintbrush. Look carefully around the ship where it touches the water; the shrinkage of the paste as it dried may have caused a concave meniscus to form that will need filling with a bit more paste. Don't get too enthusiastic about the size of the waves. Bear in mind that a wave that is only 5mm high in 1/700 scale, will represent something 3.5 metres tall in real life, and that's getting on for 12 feet

▲ I have finished modelling the waves and have painted the basic colour of the sea, mixing the paints that I showed earlier. The ship is supposed to be in the Mediterranean, where the sun will be bright and high in the sky. This means that a dark and relatively blue colour is appropriate. In the colder and overcast conditions of the North Atlantic or North Sea, a paler, greyer and perhaps greener colour would be more

convincing. Around the ship, in the wake and bow waves, where the water is agitated and foaming, I have painted it a colour that is lighter and brighter, and both greener and bluer. Next time you are on a ferry, look over the side and you will see what I mean. This lighter colour was also used on the tops of the waves, and a darker colour worked into the troughs between them

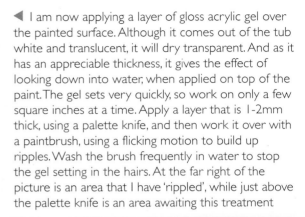

◀ I am now applying a layer of gloss acrylic gel over the painted surface. Although it comes out of the tub white and translucent, it will dry transparent. And as it has an appreciable thickness, it gives the effect of looking down into water, when applied on top of the paint. The gel sets very quickly, so work on only a few square inches at a time. Apply a layer that is 1-2mm thick, using a palette knife, and then work it over with a paintbrush, using a flicking motion to build up ripples. Wash the brush frequently in water to stop the gel setting in the hairs. At the far right of the picture is an area that I have 'rippled', while just above the palette knife is an area awaiting this treatment

▶ One of the final stages is putting white paint down to imitate foam and bubbles. I use acrylic white paint. Firstly, very dilute paint will help to emphasise the areas that I have already painted lighter, and look like water with a lot of subsurface bubbles. Don't put it on in even or thick layers, and use a small brush. Try to use multiple spots, blobs and squiggles, in a pattern that tends to follow the direction of the waves, but without looking too organised. As you go on, you can use paint that is less dilute, which will represent the foam that is on the surface. I have tried not to end up with areas that are evenly or intensely white, as these will lack the appearance of fluidity and motion

◀ This is the stern-wash, churned by the screws. I made the texture by placing the palette knife flat onto the wet layer of acrylic gel after it had been laid, and lifting it off, sharply upwards. This gave a sharp and random effect. I painted it in much the same way as the rest of the wake, but used rather more undiluted paint. You may wish to finish the sea off with a coat of clear varnish. This is controversial, as some people say that it makes the sea look too glossy. As I always spray the ship with a final coat of matt varnish, any overspray would be equally unrealistic, so I always varnish the sea as the very final stage of building the model. Maybe satin varnish might be the ideal answer

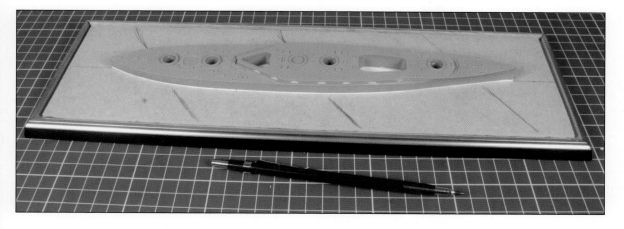

AN OCEAN SWELL

The foregoing method is fine for a ship moving through a relatively calm sea. But in the middle of the Atlantic, a ship will be confronted with an ocean swell. This is not just waves being driven by the wind, but the whole body of the water moving up and down. To imitate this you need to introduce some distortion into the overall shape of the base.

My good friend Jim Baumann is one of the finest ship modellers in the world. I would argue that actually he is THE best, in this genre at least. He is far better than me. He uses watercolour paper to make a swell, either light or heavy, and has generously shared his methods on the Internet.

I should like to demonstrate something fairly close to his method by starting a base for my next

▲ I have temporarily fixed the hull to the base so that the surface of the sea can be built up around it. It will still be possible to remove the hull to finish the model. Note that I have deepened the waterline hull by gluing a thick sheet of plasticard to the underside. This is so that I will be able to show a small amount of the underside in the troughs between the waves. It has also enabled me to bolt the hull to the base through the holes for the turret barbettes. I will just have to make sure that I don't glue the turrets in place before the rest of the completed model is finally fixed in place. The pencil lines are to show where I am going to build up the swell

project, HMS *Agincourt*. To give an idea of what this method can achieve, I should like to show you photos of the work of Werner de Keersmaecker, from Belgium.

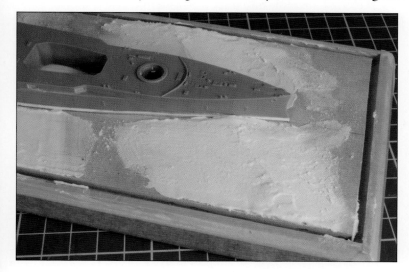

◄ I have built up the rough shape of the swelling ocean with bands of Polyfilla. The raised areas should extend as close as possible to the edge of the base, but any gaps can be filled at a later stage. I have also tried to avoid the filler touching the hull, so that it may easily be removed. When it is totally solid, I will sand down any sharp lumps or irregularities that might force their way through the watercolour paper that is going to be glued over it. Notice the masking tape that is protecting the gilding on the frame.

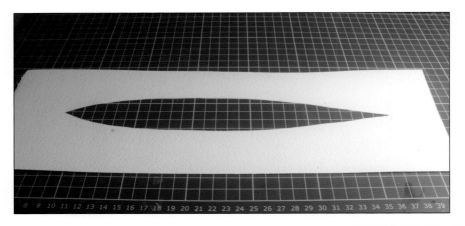

◀ 'Here's something I prepared earlier.' A sheet of watercolour paper just slightly larger than the base, with a hole the same shape as the hull's waterline. This has been cut just a fraction oversize, so that it can be eased over the hull. Any gaps between the paper and the hull will be filled in later

▶ I soaked the paper in warm water for ten to fifteen minutes in order to soften it and make it malleable. During this time I brushed a generous layer of PVA glue onto the base and all over the Polyfilla. The paper was taken out of the water and excess patted off with a towel. The damp paper was now softer and a bit stretchy. It was eased over the hull and pressed down. A little gentle persuasion was needed to stop it lifting while the glue dried. It is probable that it would have taken a lot more distortion than I have given it, but I only wanted to show an average swell, not a full blown storm

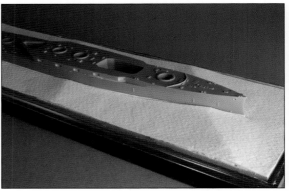

▼ Werner de Keersmaecker displayed this diorama of a U-boat at Telford in 2012. He says that he follows Jim Baumann's method exactly. Be that as it may, I don't think I have ever seen a better treatment of water. In this model Werner has managed to 'out-Baumann' Baumann. That is my honest opinion, and I think Jim was inclined to agree. Werner has been much more courageous than me in the amount of distortion that he has managed to work into the paper. I suspect that if you try a thinner grade of paper, while sticking to the rough finish, it will respond well to soaking and stretching. (This photo and the next three by WERNER DE KEERSMAECKER)

▶ You can get a view of the bows in this photo. The splashing effect can be achieved by using small pieces of torn toilet tissue. These can be glued to the base with PVA, stiffened with cyanoacrylate, and thickened and built up with white paint and acrylic gel

▲ I am amazed every time I look at this photo, and the one following. I find the effect of the wash and the foam so realistic, that the methods used to achieve it are hidden from obvious view. Understandably, Werner is not giving it all away. The streams of water running down from the limber holes seem to be multiple layers of acrylic gel, with the admixture of some streaks of white paint. In the build-up of foam around the waterline, I suspect there is some fibrous material, maybe toilet tissue soaked to disintegration and then dried out. This then graduates into a more subtle foam effect, which looks like multiple coats of very dilute white and grey-green paint, applied randomly with a stippling action. You can also notice the crew members, trying to rescue a colleague who is in danger of being washed overboard.

◀ If I look carefully at the extreme edge of the wash, I think I can see a bit more torn tissue being worked in, but it is carefully and subtly disguised, as I cannot see an inner edge. Look at all four photos, and observe the variety of different hues in the water, browns, greens, blues and greys. This does not look like ordinary acrylic paint, and I wonder if Werner has used artist's oils. I am certainly going to try experimenting with them when I pull that U-boat or Flower Class corvette out from my stash. All in all, I take my hat off to you, Werner

This is another U-boat, in larger scale by Guido Hopp. Here the swell is much heavier, and it has been built up using plaster or wall filler. Multiple thin layers have been used to avoid the problems of excessive shrinkage during drying. This will be a time consuming process. Then the water running from the deck and limber holes was done with acrylic gel. (PHOTO BY GUIDO HOPP)

The agitated area around the boat has been painted in a brighter and greener colour than the main mass of water. This model was built a few years ago, and the acrylic gel has unfortunately discoloured somewhat, taking on a yellowish hue, which is most evident on the top of the wave that the boat is ploughing through. (PHOTO BY GUIDO HOPP)

CHAPTER 7

COMBAT SITUATIONS

The primary function of a warship is to fight, whether that is against other warships, aircraft or land targets. So what better subject for a diorama could there be than to show ships engaged in combat? This sounds a very reasonable idea, and is tempting to most of us at some time in our modelling careers. But I would counsel caution, for one reason, if no other. Distance.

I have seen a number of combat dioramas on the Internet, where you have *Hood* and *Bismarck* on a single base, half a ship's length apart, guns trained on each other, and clouds of cotton wool smoke. Or a surfaced U-boat almost in contact with the ship that it is trying to torpedo.

On an Internet forum there is often no way of telling the age of the modeller. It may well have been that these were built by twelve-year-old boys. If that is so, then I would be reluctant to criticise too much and diminish their enthusiasm for the hobby. However, if they were built by grown men, I honestly think that they ought to know better.

When we make a diorama, we have to get all the components onto a single base, and also to make it a satisfying artistic composition. Since the middle of the nineteenth century, naval combat has taken place at increasingly greater ranges, until airpower and radar enabled fleets to fight while they were out of visual contact.

To take an example, let us look at the Battle of the River Plate. According to the plans of the battle issued by His Majesty's Stationery Office, the distances between *Graf Spee* and the elements of the British squadron during the battle started off at 8½ miles, closing to a minimum of five miles. If we reduce this to 1/700 scale, five miles would equate to thirty-eight feet between the vessels; hardly a practical diorama. You could reduce the scale, but if you took it down to three feet across, the ships would only be an inch long, and the vast majority of the diorama would still be blank water. If you distort things by keeping the ships at a convenient scale but contract the distances between them, then you are well on your way to making the

ludicrous *Hood/Bismarck* confrontation that I mentioned above.

So my point is that making a combat diorama that shows both points of view, and allows you to look at it from all sides, is impractical except for those occasions where combat is taking place at very close quarters. Such situations do happen. One could suggest USS *Laffey* engaging the Japanese battleship *Hiei*, where they came within twenty feet or so of each other. British readers might prefer to consider HMS *Glowworm* in collision with the German cruiser *Hipper*. And there are also those times when submarines were sunk by being rammed by surface ships.

Apart from such specific situations, the depiction of modern naval combat in a conventional diorama is problematic. We have to use a bit of imagination or lateral thinking to get around this problem.

One solution is to look at the confrontation from the point of view of one side only. A ship in battle is going to have a lot of activity, gun crews, bridge personnel, damage control parties, etc. If you have the armament trained in one particular direction, with the rangefinders and other fire control apparatus doing the same, and the attention of the crew members on the bridge following suit, then you are telling an effective story. Sure, the enemy is not being depicted on the same base that the model is sitting on, but you know that he is there. Depending on the scale that you are working in, he may be in the next room, so to speak, or across the street in your neighbour's living room. But by the way you have shown your ship, you have made the audience aware of his presence. The enemy may also be upstairs, if you have shown a ship evading and fighting off an attack from a dive bomber or *kamikaze* aircraft.

Large ships, battleships, cruisers or carriers, would operate with too much space between them to place more than one on the same base without a visually unsatisfying expanse of empty water. But with small vessels, especially torpedo boats, this idea would be entirely possible. It might be just possible to pull off the idea of two destroyers steaming together into an attack.

What about using landing craft, either circling close to their attack transport waiting for the last ones to load with troops and be lowered, or heading towards the beach in close quarters. As I write this, I am reminded of the tragedy of 'Exercise Tiger' at Slapton Sands, where German E-boats got amongst a convoy practising for D Day. I do not know how close the German boats got to the American ships,

but one may be inspired or moved to try and depict the horror and panic of a sinking LST.

In the chapter on forced perspective I shall describe the techniques for fooling the eye and brain into thinking that distances in a model are much greater than they really are. You can use this idea for combat situations as well, but with some reservations. Consider the Battle of the River Plate once more. One could have a box containing HMS *Ajax* in 1/700 scale and HMS *Achilles* in a much smaller scale. I would suggest that a commercially available 1/1200 model would probably still be too large, and that some scratch-building skills would be needed. *Graf Spee* and, depending on the time depicted, maybe *Exeter* too would also be in the picture. But at the historical ranges, both ships would be dots on the horizon. Even with forced perspective

This is HMS *Kingston* by Mike McCabe. This is the idea of a diorama showing one side of the fight. The little SM 79 aircraft are mounted on wires, and I don't think they form a permanent or integral part of the diorama. But you will notice the way that the direction that the guns point draws your attention to the enemy. See the way the ship is heeling as she turns. A ship, as opposed to a speedboat or jet-ski, will heel outwards from the direction of turn. If we go by our experience of how we ride bicycles, we might expect the heel to be inwards, but the forces and the physical principles are entirely different. (Photo by Mike McCabe)

The same diorama from a different angle. Notice the way Mike has dropped the splinter shields around the quad 0.5" machine gun. A few years ago I made a model of the destroyer USS *Hughes* in a similar situation. I think Mike's model shows it better, as the colour scheme on the *Hughes* made it somewhat difficult to see the details. (Photo by Mike McCabe)

they would still need to be shown as mere dots on the horizon.

I shall now show you a further idea for combat dioramas, using depth. Having a surface ship and a submerged submarine enables one to have two combatants close together, separated not by any horizontal distance, but by a relatively small vertical distance.

USS CHAMPLIN AND U-130

On 12 March 1943, USS *Champlin*, DD-601, a Benson Class destroyer, sank *U-130*, a Type IX U-boat. The destroyer tried to ram the U-boat, and then threw depth charges into the spot where it had crash dived. The diorama is intended to show the moment when the destroyer passes over the U-

boat, just as the depth charges are about to be launched. I have not attempted to show the depth charges being dropped or thrown, as at this instance I suspect they would either be in mid-air, or hidden in the surface of the water. That's my excuse for taking the easy way out!

I am using the Dragon kit of USS *Laffey/Woodworth*, using the *Woodworth* after superstructure but changing the armament fit to show two twin 40mm mountings. The U-boat is a Hobby Boss Type IX, a kit similar in construction and parts breakdown to the Gato and Balao submarines in the earlier chapter. I will not say anything much about the construction of the ships. There is really nothing special that I have done, aside from using the bottoms of the hulls, and I really do not want to bore you by repetition.

▶ In contrast to my usual practice, I am starting this diorama with the construction of the box. What we have here is a base with a background wall attached, made from MDF. A surround made from picture frame moulding goes around the base. The rebate in the moulding is flush with the rear vertical side, but I have left a gap, a touch over 2mm wide, between the frame and the base at the front and sides. This is to accommodate the transparent plastic sides of the box. I have put a couple of scraps of this plastic into the slots to show what I mean. The base is 23cm wide by 15cm deep, and the back is 20cm high. There is nothing magical about those dimensions

◀ Here I am pretending to be a great watercolour artist! This is watercolour paper that will be the background, and I have stretched it on a sheet of thick MDF. This is a technique for ensuring the paper stays perfectly flat and does not cockle when paint is applied. The paper is soaked in water for a couple of minutes. It is then laid flat on the board and smoothed out. The edges are fixed down with gummed paper strips. Don't try to use ordinary sticky tape. It is left at ordinary room temperature overnight. As the water evaporates, the paper first distorts and then finally dries taut and flat, giving a perfect surface for painting. There you go, another art lesson! The sheet of paper is large enough to go from the top of the back board to the front to the base, following a smooth curve

▲ This is how to paint the background. I've had this watercolour paint-box for donkey's years, and never really learned how to use it. When I get invited onto *Desert Island Discs* I may well choose it as my luxury, along with a never-ending supply of paper. I applied a graduated wash over the paper, starting with a transparent and fairly pale blue at the top, and getting much darker, thicker and more opaque the lower down it goes. The bottom half of the paper, which will cover the base, and represents the ocean depths, can be almost black. This is at least my second attempt at painting this. For the first go I applied the paint with one of the large wash brushes that you see, and I did not get a totally smooth finish. So I went over to using the airbrush. It took multiple coats of paint, which were dried with a hairdryer to speed things along, in order to get the dark and opaque effect with watercolour, which is essentially transparent. When I had finally finished, the lower part of the paper was considerably darker than is shown in this photo. Ignore the black spot, it is just a speck of dirt on the camera lens

▲ Ooops! Spot the deliberate mistake! What happened here is that I glued the background to the back of the box too far down. When I tried to form a smooth curve for the transition to the horizontal, it was too sharp and a kink or fold appeared. This was not going to be acceptable, so I had to paint a complete new background. When I fitted this one, I made sure that I used glue only on the top of the backboard and the front of the base, and ended up with a gentle curve

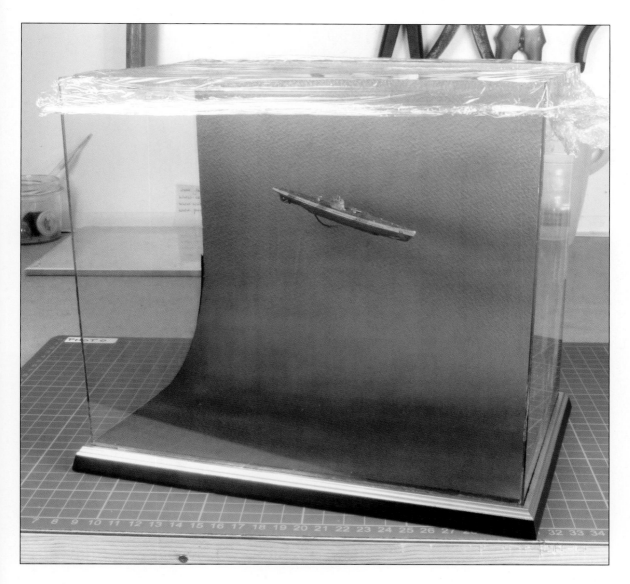

▲ Now we are getting somewhere. Before the U-boat is mounted in the box, it must be totally finished, fully painted and weathered, and photo-etch and rigging completed satisfactorily. Before gluing the hull together, I filled it with Milliput, in order to have something solid to drill into to hold the wire that mounts the U-boat onto the backboard. I considered that I would probably be looking at the final diorama with my eyes about 10cm above the water surface and at a distance of about 45cm from where the destroyer would be positioned. I therefore bent the wire so that it would be hidden by the U-boat when my eyes were in this ideal viewing position. In this photo, however, you can just get a glimpse of the wire. It has been painted dark blue to make it less conspicuous. The sides of the box have been constructed from 1.5mm sheets of a plastic called PETG. This is much clearer than polystyrene, and far easier to cut than Perspex or acrylic. It is glued using a solvent called Plastic Weld, which contains methylene chloride. This is thoroughly vile stuff. It instantly ruins any brush with which it comes into contact. I have covered the open top with Cling-Film to keep out any dust or bits of rubbish. The last thing I want is to get everything finally sealed, and realise that I am gazing at a cat hair in mid-Atlantic!

▲ This is the destroyer, again almost totally finished. It has been weathered and rigged according to my usual methods, which I described in detail in my previous book. You did buy it, didn't you? Now, it's confession time. I hold my hands up to the rivet counters, and admit my sins. The *Champlin* was one of the final Benson Class ships, and I was sitting for a couple of months with photos of her in front of me and totally failed to notice that she was built without scuttles in the fo'c'sle. By the time I realised, it was far too late to make any changes. Ho-hum, these things happen

▲ I have got another piece of PETG and cut a hole to take the destroyer. The ship has been glued in using two-part epoxy. Any gaps at the waterline have been filled with the acrylic gel that I am using to texture the underside of the water surface. The plastic has been painted blue/grey on the upper surface. This means that it is now opaque. This under surface now needs to have texture and painting for the ship's wake. I painted this in white, but I'm now not sure if a wake looks white when viewed from below

▲ Here I am doing the same thing to the upper surface. I apply a thin layer of acrylic gel with a palette knife. I only do a few square inches at a time, as it dries very quickly. Then I go over the gel with a paintbrush, making random shapes of waves and ripples with a flicking action. The brush needs to be washed out frequently with water to stop it hardening. When this first layer has set, I will go over it again, building up a few larger waves where appropriate and also the bow waves of the ship

▼ Looking down on the diorama from a somewhat steeper angle than I intended. The destroyer is showing a strip of her underwater hull as she heels out from the turn she is making. Once again it is just possible to see the wire that supports the submarine

▲ I surmised that if the Captain knew that a submarine was under the surface, and might be manoeuvring, he would want his guns to give optimum coverage of all angles of the horizon. Hence the forward 5'' guns being trained at 45° on either bow, and the after guns doing the same on each quarter. I have put plenty of figures on the deck, but every one has been positioned with a purpose in mind.

▲ The mounting wire cannot be seen now. I have positioned the photographic lights so that they cancel out the shadows cast by each other. The U-boat really does look as though it is hanging in the water

CHAPTER 8

SMALL IS BEAUTIFUL

This is going to be a very short chapter. That is because it is about a very small subject. It is simply a plea from the heart not to forget little things.

When we see a collection of models on a club or competition table, the natural reaction is to pay attention to the largest and most obviously impressive ones. There is a cynical joke about how best to win an IPMS club contest. Make something big, and paint it orange!

But hidden away in the shadows may be something exquisite and tiny, and this is just as worthy, perhaps more so, because it is not yelling out about itself.

▼ This diorama is only three inches square across the water surface. It is one of the Elco PT boats that served in the Philippines in 1942, and were the inspiration for the John Wayne film *They Were Expendable*. It is a 1/350 scale resin kit by MS Models of St Petersburg. I have never seen another kit by this company and it may be that it was the only thing they produced. That would be a pity, as the moulding is of the most exquisite quality

▲ Despite the small size of the diorama, I have managed to incorporate a lot of activity, without it feeling cramped. There are men doing something, I know not what, in the whaleboat, the pile of stores, officers on the jetty talking to the boat's commander, and men fixing the Lewis gun onto its mounting, not to mention the guy fishing! The jetty was made from individual plastic strips for the planks, as you can see by the irregularities at the end.

There is probably something cultural going on here. I am a Brit. Compared to our American cousins, we live on a small island. It is crowded and we don't have much space. In common with other Europeans, we drive small cars, and we live in small houses. The newer the house, the more cramped it is likely to be. This may be part of the reason that 1/700 scale ships are more popular this side of the Atlantic. And I am certainly drawn to the tiniest things on the table.

A good small diorama requires a somewhat different approach from a large one. A large diorama can make a bold statement and be viewed from a distance. It is sometimes possible, though not advisable, to be less precise in the work that is on the periphery and away from the main points of interest. Metaphorically speaking, you can paint with a big brush and broad strokes.

But a small diorama is different. It beckons to you and whispers quietly, saying, 'Come here. Bend down. Look at me. Look at me really closely. Examine me.' Being short-sighted, I will take my glasses off, put my Optivisor on, and get

to within six inches. At this distance, and with the whole diorama still within my field of vision, nothing is hidden.

Every part of the diorama is going to be close to the main point of interest, and therefore care must be lavished upon all of them. You will be looking at it sufficiently closely to be aware of every messy brushstroke and every speck of dust. Small dioramas may not be easier than large ones; they may actually be more challenging. But don't let that put you off. The dress that your wife is wearing may be beautiful; but then so is the tiny ring on her finger.

▲ This photo, and the two following, show the most delightful small diorama that I have ever seen. It is by Mike McCabe again, and shows the Argentinian aviso *General Comandante Zapiola* visiting a scientific station in Tierra del Fuego. This one too is only three inches square, but it punches above its weight in storytelling and emotion. It really speaks to me of isolation and loneliness, wistful yearning for home, and a constant struggle to survive in a harsh environment. Mike has even managed to include some seagulls and dolphins in the composition. I admire this model every time I see it. (PHOTOS BY MIKE MCCABE)

CHAPTER 9

'THE WRONG END OF THE TELESCOPE' – FORCED PERSPECTIVE

We live in a three dimensional world. I know that if you are a physicist, or an expert in quantum mechanics, you may well insist that there are numerous extra dimensions and an infinite number of parallel universes, but for us mere mortals, the traditional three dimensions of length, breadth and height have always been sufficient.

Our senses, or some of them at least, have various ways of giving us information about our position in our environment and our spatial relationships with other objects around us. For example, touch. As I sit here typing at the computer, if I move my hand from the keyboard to touch the VDU screen, then the sensations from my finger and the movement that my arm makes tell me that the screen is further away from me. Likewise, the sound of the car outside the window, getting louder and then softer again, indicates that it is driving towards me and then moving away in the opposite direction. These are so fundamental to our experience of life that we do not think about them at all.

When we are examining models, the most important sense that we use is our sight, and this gives us more three dimensional information than the others. Let's take a moment to consider how sight conveys the idea of distance to the mind.

STEREOSCOPY AND PARALLAX

We have two eyes, separated by about three inches. Each one sees a slightly different image of the world that it transmits to the brain, and the brain then uses the two sets of information to build up a composite picture that includes evidence of depth or distance. This is stereoscopic vision. With one eye closed it becomes more difficult to estimate how far away objects are, though it is by no means impossible.

To demonstrate this idea of slightly different images from each eye, close one eye, hold your thumb up in front of you at arm's length, and use it to cover an object in the distance, say something on the wall opposite. Now open that eye and close the other. The hidden object will appear to jump out from behind your thumb.

Stereoscopy is closely related to the phenomenon of parallax. If I move my head to the right, and look at the relative positions of two objects, one close and the other more distant, then the distant object appears to move to the right, in the same direction as my head, and the closer object seems to move to the left. Similar and corresponding shifts occur if I move my head in the other direction and also up or down.

RELATIVE SIZE

The further away an object is from the eye the smaller it appears. Take two identical pens, place one on a table at the opposite end of the room and hold the other in your hand. You didn't even have to do that to realise that the pen on the table would seem smaller, even though you knew both were exactly the same size.

Or stand in the middle of a straight stretch of road, preferably traffic free! The sides of the road appear to converge as it recedes into the distance. This is how you know that it is actually going away from you.

This is the idea behind the principle of linear perspective, of which more will be written shortly.

Less in the way of small features and detail can be seen on distant objects. Hence the phrase, 'Don't shoot until you can see the whites of their eyes!'

ATMOSPHERIC PERSPECTIVE

The air is full of water vapour and particulate matter. Light reflected off objects and coming to our eyes is disturbed by this vapour, and the further it has to travel, the more it is affected.

The result of this is that distant objects appear to be lighter in tone and bluer in hue. If you are lucky enough to have a good view from the window, look outside. The distant horizon, even if you know that it is covered with trees, will be seen to be shades of pale blue and grey.

Alternatively, go to a newly built housing estate. The houses will be largely identical, with exactly the same bricks and roof tiles. But the bricks and tiles on the house that is close to you will look much darker, warmer and richer than on a distant house. You know in your conscious mind that the materials are the same, but they look different.

A view across the River Clyde towards Dumbarton and beyond. The photo is two dimensional. It has been printed on flat paper. But our brain lets us interpret it as an image of something three dimensional. The trees in the foreground are larger than those on the other side of the river. You cannot see individual branches on those distant trees. And the colours become paler the further away things get, until the most distant mountains are almost indistinguishable from the clouds

These are the basic phenomena that enable us to find our way about in a three dimensional world. They are not tricks; they are simply a description of the way that the laws of physics and mathematics impinge on our minds.

Knowledge of how these phenomena operate can be used to trick the eye. Artists have been doing it for hundreds of years, refining their techniques ever since the start of the Renaissance in the fifteenth century. If you look at any competent landscape painting, you will see how artists are able to give the impression of three dimensions on a flat and two dimensional canvas.

As you stand and look at the picture, perhaps six feet in front of you, every image painted on the canvas is very nearly the same distance from your eye. But the images of objects that you know to be the same size in reality, people for example, are painted in various sizes. You interpret the larger and more detailed images as being the foreground, and the smaller ones as being more distant, further down the road. Of course, it might just be possible, though very unlikely, that the artist intends us to think that the small human image is actually a doll, in the foreground, suspended in the air by magic. But the eye, lacking the extra information that parallax would offer, makes the natural assumption that it is a full sized human standing by the roadside in the distance.

Similarly, the images of trees that are painted in full, rich, warm and dark colours are interpreted as

being relatively close, while those that are paler and bluer are much more distant.

So, what has this got to do with modelling? An artist is able to fool the eye into thinking that a two dimensional canvas is actually a three dimensional world. Are we not also artists, in our own way? It is entirely possible for modellers to use these same types of illusions and spatial distortions to make distances appear much greater in our models than they really are. This is what 'forced perspective' is all about.

The basic principle is one of combining models of different scales, larger in front and smaller behind, and restricting the angle from which the arrangement can be viewed. This makes the distances between the models appear much greater than they actually are.

If you take a 1/350 scale model and look at it from a comfortable distance of two feet, this will be equivalent to looking at the full size vessel from 700 feet away (2 x 350).

Now take a 1/700 model and place it six inches behind the larger one, so that it is 2ft 6in from your eye. This will now be equivalent to a full size vessel 1,750 feet away (2.5 x 700).

Take a third model, this time 1/1400 scale and place it again six inches behind the second one, so that it is three feet from your eye. This tiniest model will look like a full size vessel 4,200 feet away (3 x 1,400).

The distance between the front and back models is one foot, equivalent to 350 feet if you scale up from the front model. By using this trick it will seem as though the models are actually separated by 3,500 feet (4,200 – 700). You have succeeded in stretching the distance by a factor of 10.

But keep your eyes in this one spot. Don't move your head from side to side or try to look at the models from a different direction. If you do the illusion will be totally lost. When you look at the arrangement from the back you will think that the sailors on the largest vessel are playing with their radio-controlled boats!

Because of this need to restrict the angle from which the models can be viewed, it is essential that forced perspective is done in the context of a box diorama, with a small window in the front. Lighting can be fitted, using small electric bulbs or LEDs. A subtly painted background sets everything off.

I have so far just mentioned playing tricks with relative size and parallax to fool the eye. You can use the idea of atmospheric perspective, also known to modellers as 'scale colour' as well. If you add increasing proportions of white or pale grey to the paint mixtures that you use as the scales get smaller, this will increase the illusion of distance. It will also drive the 'Colour Police' on the judging panels totally mental, and that is another great advantage!

Before I get on to the process of describing how I built 'The Hunting Party', there are a few other observations that I feel it is important to make. Firstly, from a purely practical point of view, a box diorama is best suited to models that are small in overall size. The Hunting Party uses PT boats, and this is an ideal choice. It would also be possible to use a 1/700 destroyer, or at a pinch, a 1/350 corvette. But if you try making the front vessel a 1/350 battleship or carrier, the resulting box would be so enormous that transport would require a medium sized van, at least. Such an ambitious project would need to be planned as a permanent display in a museum setting.

Because the models are only going to be looked at from one side, then there is no real need to expend too much effort on finishing the backs to the same standard as the fronts. What is going to be visible needs the best quality of work that you are capable of, but on the other hand there is certainly no need to paint a complicated disruptive or dazzle camouflage pattern on areas that will not be seen. In fact, if you wanted to really make a point, you could leave bare plastic!

By the same token, I would suggest that if you used incredibly highly detailed models in a box diorama, it would be a waste. If you have expended months on a model, doing the most exquisite photo-etch work, rigging and weathering, then it really deserves to be appreciated from all angles and from as close as your vision will allow. Put this one on its own pedestal, and use something a bit simpler in the box.

'THE HUNTING PARTY'

The basic concept of the diorama is of a squadron of American PT boats departing on a patrol fairly late in the war. I chose this subject because of the ready availability of kits of Elco PT boats in both 1/350 and 1/700 scales. I used the kits from White

Ensign. Although they are eighty feet boats, they represent Kennedy's *PT 109*, and therefore have a different configuration to the later, more heavily armed boats. Some conversion was needed to change the deck fittings, machine gun tub position, replacement of the torpedo tubes with roll-off racks and adding 40mm, 37mm and 20mm guns, as well as rocket launchers. The 40mm guns were highly detailed resin parts from Niko. Actually, that wasn't 'some' conversion work; it was really quite a lot!

The 1/1400 boats were scratch-built from scraps of plastic. It was only necessary to give a basic outline, as a highly detailed replica would have been out of place and upset the sense of perspective.

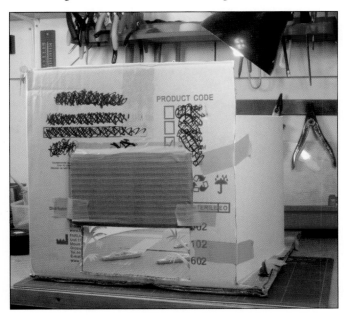

◄ This shows part of the planning process. Before doing any significant construction, I had to ensure that the concept would work. I had to answer the questions of the size of box that I needed, how large or small the front window should be, how the background should be shaped and how far forward it should extend so that the viewer could not see the front edges. The box would also have to be high enough to hide any lighting and also the top edge of the background. Most importantly, I had to convince myself that the arrangement of the boats would give a convincing effect of receding into the distance. This is, of course, just part of a cardboard packing case, with a semicircular background roughly fitted inside, and a viewing window cut out of the front. The extra piece of cardboard enables me to experiment with different sizes of openings

▲ Another view of the same, showing the background, made out of two pieces of watercolour paper. This process of working out sizes and checking sight-lines is vital. Because I do not want to see any 'seams' in the sky, the final background will be cut from one single sheet of watercolour paper, with a maximum length of thirty-three inches. As it curves around the inside of the box, the front edges will not reach right to the front. By doing this preliminary work, I can be happy that the viewing window is small enough so that the edges will not be visible under normal circumstances.

Also note how close together the different boats are, from front to rear. In the final diorama this will be about nine inches. It is a little closer that the mathematical example that I worked out above, but will still give an apparent separation of 3,500 feet when the viewer's eye is two feet from the largest boat

▲ This is a view through the front window. Already you can see how the effect of distance is being achieved. I have drawn a rough outline of an island on the background. In this experiment I put the cut-outs of palm trees in the same plane that the window glass will occupy. I toyed with the idea of some 1/72 figures there too, watching from the shore. Although this would have added quite a lot to the effect of perspective, I chose not to pursue it, as it would have made the front boats appear to be far too close to the beach.

The viewing window must be situated as low down as possible, and fairly small, particularly in the vertical dimension. This is to make the viewer feel that he is on the same level as the action of the diorama. The boats furthest away must be seen behind the closer boats, not over them. That would spoil the effect. Also, the more you can look down on the scene, the more you will notice the curve of the background horizon. It is possible to see a little of this already

▶ Here are the boats with their basic paint jobs done. This photo reminds me why I wanted late war boats. It was not just because of the heavy armament; it was more because of the really cool colour scheme. And this leads me to underline two important points. The largest boats are painted with full strength colours, and the black areas of the scheme are done in very dark grey. The

others have had increasing proportions of light grey added to the mix so that the smallest boats are done in a washed-out light green, and the black is actually

no more than a mid-grey. And look at the port sides of the boats. These will not be seen, so I have not wasted any time on painting a scheme here at all

◀ This is the box for the diorama. It is made from 6mm MDF. When it is finished, it will have a clear plastic lid to keep out dust, but let light in. The sea base is also cut from MDF, with a curved shape that the background can fit neatly behind, thus avoiding gaps or shadows at the horizon. The base has had a sheet of watercolour paper glued to it and the sea painted with watercolour paints. Note that the colour is much fuller and darker at the front and gets paler towards the rear. This is to copy the real appearance of the sea. Close to you, where you look down at it, the sea looks dark and the colour you expect, but towards the horizon it is much paler, and only a shade or two darker than the sky. The background is similarly painted with watercolour paints, in a 'graduated wash'. Please do not comment on my lousy skills as a watercolour artist. It may be a particularly British art form, but that doesn't mean we're all good at it!

◀ The boats are now glued to the base. Waves, sea texture and wakes have been built up using acrylic gel, torn up scraps of toilet paper and white paint. The texture of the sea surface has been confined almost exclusively to the areas around and in front of the largest boats. The areas further away received little more than a coat of varnish

▶ I know I've been banging on about only looking at a forced perspective diorama from one direction. This photo shows you why. It now looks like playtime with model boats, or the USN in hot pursuit of the Lilliputian Navy! Nevertheless, it always amazes me what a high proportion of grown, and presumably sensible men look in through the lid, which has been obscured to prevent it, and go, 'Hhhmmm', rather than use the window at the front. It's the six-year-old boys who get the idea straight off

▶ We are now getting towards a completed diorama. The base is glued permanently into the box, as is the background. I have also fitted LEDs for additional lighting. Although the transparent lid will let in a fair amount of light, extra lighting is required to enhance the perspective effect. If you recall school physics lessons when you learned about the 'Inverse Square Law', you will realise that those elements that have most illumination will appear to be closest. The lighting is therefore

concentrated on the front half of the box. I chose the LEDs carefully, because they emit their light in a precise beam, and sometimes this is narrow. I did not want lots of spots of light, and so I got wide-angle LEDs, with beam of about 135°. With careful positioning, this flooded the front half of the box with light

▲ The LEDs are lit. The little plastic holders are held in position with double-sided tape, and the terminal wires bent to direct the light where it is wanted. LEDs have a precise range of current within which they will work. Too

little and they won't light at all; too much and they blow. So the circuit is a bit complicated. They are wired in groups of four. The LEDs in each group are in series with a suitable resistor to moderate the current that will be provided by the 12-volt battery. The four groups of four are then wired in parallel, with a simple push switch in the circuit. I know that is as clear as mud, but if you Google 'LED circuit', you will find the answer better than I can explain. You will also notice that I changed my mind once again during construction, and the front window has been reduced in size, to further control the angle from which the diorama can be viewed

▶ The power source, a simple 12-volt rechargeable battery, which I found lying around the house. Make sure that it is connected the right way round. I believe that LEDs will blow if the current flows the wrong way. Replacing them all will be an expensive pain in the neck

◀ A transparent lid is essential to let light into the box. Unfortunately, it also allows grown men to peer in. Hence the scumbled white paint to partly obscure the view. It still doesn't work. They still try to look straight down into it! I'm going to have to put a little label there, saying 'For ***** sake, look in the front!'

▲ Getting a satisfactory photograph through the window of this diorama is very difficult. Although it is possible to get enough illumination onto the models to appreciate them with the naked eye, the shape of the box means that it is hard, even with strong photographic lamps, to light the front of the largest boats enough for a good exposure. Also notice how the horizon appears to curve. This is due to the shape and size of the box, and is the feature of the diorama that does not work well. If I had made the box so wide that I could have had a straight background, and still not see the edges, it would have worked visually, but have been an unwieldy size

CHAPTER 10

BIG, BOLD AND ...'BLIMEY!'

This chapter is about big dioramas. Enormous, eye-boggling pieces of work, involving large numbers of ships. The sort of thing you dream about for years, and then, when you have a sudden flash of insanity, you launch into a project that you reckon will astound your friends and win numerous plaudits and even some prizes. But it is also a project that you may regret taking on before you are halfway through, or leaves you feeling disappointed or heartily fed up at the end.

So, before you start too much planning, ask yourself some very hard questions about the finished result. Basic ones, like, Why? Where? How? And most importantly, Who?

Why are you doing it? Is it for some major exhibition or commemoration? That's fine, very commendable. Or is it to satisfy an urge in your own mind? Nothing fundamentally wrong with that, either. But might your modelling urges be better satisfied by making a number of smaller individual projects, which can each be completed individually, rather than getting mired in something that grows like Topsy?

Where is it going to be built, displayed or stored? If you have your own workshop or 'playroom', the first consideration may not be a problem. But what about when it is finished? A big diorama needs a big base and a correspondingly large area for display. Is there space in your house to show it off? Or do you have the ability to store it without damage, deterioration or the accumulation of dust? So often a large diorama has to suffer the ignominy of storage under a bed, in the same way that the children's model train set is pushed away at night. This will guarantee irreparable damage in very short order, especially if you have a cat!

How will you move it? If you are a member of a modelling club, or IPMS, you will probably want to attend meetings or shows. And you will want to show off your handiwork to as many friends as possible. So are you going to be able to transport it, bearing in mind that you may want to take other people, wife or children, not to mention other models and still have room for those big purchases you make on impulse. I only have a small Vauxhall Corsa, and every year that we go to the British Nationals at Telford, I have to weigh up the practicalities of strapping my wife to the roof rack. If I also had to consider hiring a furniture van for the weekend, I'm sure I'd lose her support for my hobby.

That was also answering the 'Who?' question. Most of us have wives, girlfriends, partners, and occasionally husbands, for some modellers are women, and the needs of these other parties have to be taken into consideration. Is the other party really going to appreciate being taken over by a scale model of the whole of Pearl Harbor? Our dreams often have to be modified by the realities of family life.

Assuming you have settled these questions, it is as well to have an end point in mind, and one that is realistic. There is little point in aiming to have something finished in a year, if it is going to involve ten ships, and you know that it usually takes you two months to finish each one. You would not finish it to your satisfaction, or would make a very rushed job of it all. But on the other hand, if you enter into a big project with little idea of timescale, and something that is totally open-ended, you will tend to drift, get distracted and side-tracked by other ideas, and be much less likely to ever finish.

There is a tendency when making a large diorama to go with a quick 'big brush' approach. By this, I mean taking a large component, say the quayside, or the water surface, and doing it in a slap-dash way that would be totally unacceptable in a smaller model. I have seen dioramas where the water has been painted with a 2" house painting brush. The brush marks are obvious and any sense of reality destroyed by careless workmanship. If you were building ten individual ships, which you expect people to look at closely, you would expend time and effort on doing your best work. The same care should be given if the ships are to be combined into a single composite arrangement.

All these pitfalls come together in a memory from my teenage years, when I was a member of the Air Cadets. Our Squadron Leader was a totally ineffectual little man, with 'little man's syndrome'. His plans and ego always totally outstripped his abilities to see anything through. One day he suggested to us, 'Let's build a model of a Battle of Britain airfield.' The plan was to get a runway, hangars, control tower, dispersal area, fire engines and ambulances, not to mention an Airfix Spitfire for every member of the squadron, onto a base which would fit onto a table tennis table. It may even have involved using the table tennis table *as* the base.

Naturally, being teenage boys, everyone wanted to build an aeroplane, and nobody wanted or felt able to build a hangar, let alone a boring dispersal pen. The table had to be dismantled and stacked away every time we paraded in the clubroom, or had any other type of activity. What started out with a flash of misdirected enthusiasm, fizzled out

no more than six weeks later, in complete apathy, which in hindsight was totally predictable.

Nevertheless, large dioramas can be an ideal project for a group of like-minded modellers, provided they are all committed to the idea, and are able to work together to a common aim and deadline. People have their own different interests and specialities, and a project with a lot of disparate elements can play to everyone's particular strengths. Some people may be good at ships, others at buildings, someone else at water surfaces and yet another at organising, planning and cracking the whip.

The next section describes just such a major project.

THE LIVERPOOL DOCKS DIORAMA BY 'THE GERMAN GAMBLERS'

There is a group of friends from Germany who come to Telford most years. They call themselves 'VMF-06, The German Gamblers'. I think this title is a play on the naming and numbering of US Navy air squadrons. In their case, VMF stands for 'Virtual Modelling Friends'. Their work is always of the highest order, and they won the award for the best display by overseas visitors on at least one occasion.

In November 2008, they brought to Telford a diorama that they had built during the previous eighteen months, depicting part of Liverpool docks during the Battle of the Atlantic. It received a lot of admiring comments, and was one of the highlights of the ship-related part of the show.

At the time of completion, I believe that the final fate of the diorama had not been decided, and the baseboard at least, if not the whole diorama, was stored under a bed for a time. Fortunately, they have now found a permanent home for it, and it is displayed on board the museum ship ORP *Blyskawica* at Gdynia in Poland.

I am extremely grateful to Christian, Guido, Torben and Frank for their permission to reproduce below an article that they wrote about the building of this diorama. It explains far better than I can, the process of planning, building and bringing together, along with the pitfalls and difficulties that they had to overcome. I am also grateful for the huge number of photos that they sent, only a few of which I am able choose for publication here.

Building a Diorama of Liverpool's Langton and Brocklebank Docks

An Idea is Born

Depicting ship models in the environment we landlubbers usually get to see ships – in port – was always on my mind since I restarted building ship models in 2004. British and Canadian escorts from the Second World War have always been of interest to me; hence the project should have a British subject. Jim Baumann and Peter Fulgoney, having presented their excellent harbour dioramas in 2006, precluded choosing a similar scene in order not to wear the subject out.

By coincidence I found various plans of British docks and harbours while doing Internet research. Luckily these plans included scales, so I was able to convert the dimensions. Poring through these plans, the double access to Liverpool's Langton Docks, one of the numerous docks along the River Mersey, appealed to me ever more. Getting the measurements and converting them into 1/700 scale soon showed that a decent depiction would take up an amount of space that was hard to cope with for a single modeller in a given timeframe. But what are friends for after all, especially friends that share your interests?

In the spring of 2007 I presented my idea to my friends Frank Ilse, Guido Hopp, Dirk Mennigke and Torben Keitel. As Guido and Torben both have an anglophile strain to them, they soon agreed to cooperate on this project. Frank and Dirk prefer 1/350 scale and planned to execute a project of their own. We soon agreed that both projects complemented one another and could be presented simultaneously at our display.

As I already had a certain scene in mind, I continued research into the story we meant to tell with our diorama. Guido and Torben researched dock structures and buildings. Later on in the project, our new member Frank Spahr joined our group and the diorama project.

The Story

Each diorama has to tell a story. In our case we meant to depict how merchant vessels and escorts enter the port after completing a convoy voyage. That said, we needed to choose the timeframe, the convoy and the individual vessels involved. The excellent web resources Convoy Web and the Wuerttembergische Landesbibliothek both offer comprehensive data on naval warfare 1939-45, and here I found the necessary information to determine the composition of our diorama.

Sources:

http://www.battleships-cruisers.co.uk/royal.htm
http://www.wlb-stuttgart.de/seekrieg/konvois/konvois-frames.htm
http://www.convoyweb.org.uk/sc/index.html

The diorama was to present the situation on 4 April 1943. On this day, convoy SC.123 arrived at Liverpool with fifty merchantmen – and without losses – after sailing from New York on 14 March. From 20 March on, Escort Group B2 (home-ported at Liverpool) took part in the protection of the convoy. This group was commanded by Cdr D G MacIntyre, DSO RN; it comprised the destroyers HMS *Vanessa* and *Whitehall* as well as the corvettes HMS *Clematis*, *Gentian*, *Heather* and *Sweetbriar*. The rest of the group – the destroyer HMS *Hesperus*, the corvette HMS *Campanula* and the frigate HMS *Mourne* did not take part; they spent the time at Liverpool undergoing refits and repairs.

The diorama was to show some of the vessels already moored in port, with others in the process of entering port, depicting them in various phases of the manoeuvre. Moreover we meant to include various tugs, trawlers and other working vessels as only these really bring a port scene to life.

Building the Idea

Having agreed on the scene to depict, we needed more research into the dock structures. Guido worked hard and obtained photos and information on the Liverpool docks that gave us a fairly good idea of how these docks looked between 1929 and 1955. The section we intended to build was a part of Langton and Brocklebank Docks. Various warehouses and other buildings were identified, as well as a swivel bridge and a jetty built in front of the actual entrance to the dock.

A host of other questions had to be answered: how was the water to be simulated, how high were the quays and how were they actually constructed, and – most important of all: which items were available in kit form and which had to be scratch-built? We soon agreed on the timeframe as we wanted to present the diorama at Scale ModelWorld 2008, held in Telford on 15–16 November, 2008.

We soon knew what could be obtained in kit form and what had to be scratch-built. The quays, bridges, locks and the jetty would have to be scratch-built. Warehouses and vehicles were available from Battlefleet Models and White Ensign Models.

Before we finally were able to start, we needed to assign the work amongst the group. Frank and Torben built the only destroyer, HMS *Hesperus*, plus the corvettes HMS *Heather* and HMS *Saxifrage*. Torben also built the small swivel bridge. Guido and I divided the remaining vessels amongst us, with Guido building the Empire freighter SS *Empire Pibroch*, the corvette HMS *Clematis*, the sloop HMS *Totland* plus the trawler HMT *Kirkella*. That left me with two freighters, the Hog

Islander SS *Shikshinney* and the tramp SS *Fjordheim*; apart from that I built the corvette HMS *Campanula* and two trawlers – HMT *Indian Star* and HMT *Inkpen*. The numerous other small vessels and vehicles were set aside for the time being. Guido also undertook building the jetty, and I took care of the display itself, the docks and buildings.

Even though this diorama was a team project, most working hours were spent in our individual workshops. We held four meetings throughout the building process, yet hardly ever with all the participants being present due to work or other commitments. In the first meeting held in March 2008, we agreed on the positioning of the vessels and discussed how to fabricate the dock structures and buildings and how to simulate the water. Already it was clear that Torben would not be able to go to Telford due to professional commitments.

Building the Ship Models

The ships were built between the autumn of 2007 and the autumn of 2008; actually the last vessels were completed just in time for the presentation. As we knew which paint schemes and which equipment to use on the escorts; building them was a straightforward process. Only Frank had to do extra work on his *Hesperus*, as there is no kit of this vessel in her 1943 fit. He therefore had to kit-bash Niko Model's ORP *Garland* kit with B-Resina's HMS *Hero*. All the corvettes and sloops were built using the WEM and HP Models kits, same as the three trawlers. The trawlers are based on the HP *Vorpostenboot* V 1102 kit and received major modifications to resemble British vessels.

The Empire freighter was based on the HP Models kit, whereas the Hog Islander was built using the excellent Battlefleet Models kit. The tramp steamer is based on Loose Cannon's kit of the SS *Dayrose*. All models were detailed and improved. All resin masts were replaced with brass items. Watertight doors, hatches, vertical and inclined ladders, railings, radars, davits and the like were taken from the various photo-etched sets produced by WEM, L'Arsenal, Lion Roar and Tom's Modelworks. Various items were replaced by resin parts, such as Niko's Hedgehog launchers. Styrene stock was used for conversions, such as *Hesperus* and the trawlers. All the models were painted and weathered as per our references. With the freighters, we chose to use various shades of grey plus a peacetime scheme for the tramp.

Building the Display and the Docks

In order to keep the diorama manageable to work on and to transport, we agreed on a size of 700 × 550mm (27.56 × 21.65 inches); a rectangle of that size was overlaid on the plan and the section thus chosen and defined. We intended to keep the dock structure as simple as possible, and we were helped by the way the Liverpool docks were built. They consisted mainly of cast concrete, with their fronts lacking any of the reinforcements so commonly found. The Mersey's mean tidal range exceeds seven metres (23 feet), and this is what the docks are built for. So we decided on a visible height of 8mm (.31 inch) for the docks, which translates into 5.6 metres (18 ft 4 in) and should be correct for a median tidal range.

Making docks from 8mm styrene stock sounded easy at first, but it soon proved to be pretty hard to achieve crisp cuts in styrene of that gauge, let alone in the length needed. While discussing the issue with modelling friends the idea of computer assisted milling turned up. Coincidentally one of the friends, a freelance designer, owns a 3-axis milling machine that could make quick work of the job needed. Having already designed the docks using CAD software made conversion into *.dxf format and importing the data into the machine easy. Within a few days I had the crisply milled parts at home.

For an attractive presentation, a base plate was cut from 19mm MDF, and an ornamental frame was crafted from beech. The latter was stained and polished. The base plate was fixed to the frame with screws, enabling us to use the frame for other future projects. It was only fixed to the frame after all other work was completed.

After removing the dock parts, their edges were cleaned up lightly. To keep the whole setup flexible, the dock elements and the main buildings were to be screwed to the base. Hence, the sections were aligned, temporarily fixed to the plate, holes were drilled and threads were cut. After finally determining the buildings' positions, they were treated likewise. The prominent lock gates at the dock's entrance were scratch-built from styrene stock using photographic references. The handedness of the gates necessitated making a pattern for both a left-handed and a right-handed gate. Moulds were made from the patterns and the required number of parts was cast in resin.

Upon our second meeting in July both the base and the dock elements were completed; that made finalising the vessels' positions easier. At this meeting we decided on how to simulate the water and agreed on the further schedule. Most of the vessels built by Torben, Frank and Guido were completed at the time.

Making the Water – 3rd Meeting

Before the next meeting scheduled for early September I had to perform a lot of work on my ship models. I had already decided not to implement one of the vessels originally planned. Guido and Torben could not participate due to professional commitments, so Frank and I made the water and continued on other aspects of the diorama. Torben had visited me before to make sure the swivel bridge did fit. We realised we would have to do some adjustments to the dock to fit the bridge.

The main issue of the third meeting was making the water. We used a method Frank had successfully executed several times before. To correctly replicate the shade of the Mersey and the water in the docks – a pleasant muddy multi-hued green-brown – we consulted Google Earth's satellite view. The dock entrance still exists, even though many of the docks have been demolished or backfilled.

The first step was brush painting the base in an appropriate basic hue, using liberal amounts of wall paint stippled on to give the surface some structure replicating the ripples of the water. That cured, the contours of the docks and vessels were marked and masked. Using two airbrushes, we then applied various shades of green, grey and brown, always trying to simulate the effects caused by currents and the movements of the vessels. Vallejo's Model Air acrylics proved to be ideally suited to blend the shades nicely. After we were satisfied with the result, we sealed the entire water area with several coats of clear gloss lacquer from a rattle can, taking care not to overdo the gloss. We concluded this day's work by priming the various buildings and vehicles.

Tedious Stuff – Vehicles, Figures and Paraphernalia

Bringing a diorama to life needs many small elements. In our case this meant assorted buildings, tugs, vehicles, cargo, figures and so on. We divided this work amongst us. Frank produced assorted cargo like piles of boxes, heaps of sand and coal, winches, train engines and cars plus military goods stored on the quays. Guido built around 110 freight cars, train engines and lorries. Torben built several tugs, barges and other working vessels, and I had about fifty lorries and various cargoes on my workbench – plus the docks and buildings! Painting and weathering all this took several evenings and weekends. We only used acrylic paints; weathering was done using artist's oil paints and pastel chalks.

Having completed the docks and buildings, they could be fixed to the base, with the lacquer having had ample time for curing. A first trial using available elements and vehicles showed a need for considerably more details. So quayside lamps were made from brass wire and white glue. Moreover, a collection of cutters, barges and rowing boats were taken from numerous detail sets; they were painted, weathered and spread around the diorama. Inclined and vertical ladders as well as working rafts brought additional life to the scene.

The swivel bridge was also finally fitted and fixed to the base. On the quays, railroad tracks were marked. In the meantime, Guido worked hard on the jetty, a focal point of the diorama. The first in-progress images he sent showed extremely delicate PE structures and let my excitement mount. Guido and Frank painstakingly painted 1:700 PE figures, ending up with about 3,000 of them.

Apart from all the docks, buildings, vehicles and so on, my ship models were completed by the end of October. So the road was clear to a final meeting to complete the diorama.

4th Meeting and Completion

Frank and I met for the final building session. Having fixed the quays and main buildings, we had to add the smaller buildings, vehicles, small items and figures in lively scenes. After several rehearsals we were satisfied with the result and started fixing the elements to the base. White glue was used to keep the pieces removable, only the 300 figures were super-glued. Yes, only 300 of them. Alert readers will wonder why we left 2,700 figures out. But those 300 figures brought so much life to the scene that less seemed more. We will surely use the remaining figures someday.

To add more realism, we needed moorings and tow cables. These were made from copper wire to be as flexible in regard to the ships' positions as possible.

Fitting the delicate jetty to the quay was an exciting moment. Guido had built the parts using only the plans I had provided him, without any access to the actual parts. Nonetheless it was a perfect fit – so the CAD plans have worked well.

All the while we made travel plans for our trip to Telford. Ferry, hotel and a van had to be booked, as well as the itinerary and our registration for SMW 2008. Frank Ilse and Dirk Mennigke had almost completed their diorama project – it was two weeks to go to Scale ModelWorld.

Whereas Frank had decided to leave his vessels on the diorama, I had to make a transport box for my vessels.

Scale ModelWorld 2008

In the afternoon of 14 November, the exhibition halls were opened to set up the show. After assembling our stand, we finally were able to unpack and assemble the diorama with all the vessels. Everything fitted and went according to plan and – most important of all – as we had envisioned. Our depiction of the Liverpool docks was easily recognisable and more than a few visitors said, 'These are Liverpool Docks, aren't they?' We very much appreciated that, as it showed that we had replicated the original in a fair way.

Conclusion

We can but confirm what Frank Ilse and Dirk Mennigke related to us after building their Pacific diorama – the commitment and the number of hours needed to complete such a project is considerable. We did not count the hours, but it must have been several hundred of them. Originally we had thought it would not matter if we did not complete the project on time; but at some point, upon realising the amount of work still needed, we got caught by an ambition to nonetheless get things done on time. Considering our professional and private commitments, this is anything but simple, and it must not be forgotten that scale modelling is a hobby (or is at least supposed to be . . .)

Realising this project presented fresh experiences to us all. Most important to me was to learn that it is possible to build a common project with four individuals, all of them with opinions and perspectives of their own, even though separated by several hundred miles and with phone and email as the main communication tools. That needs discipline, commitment, mutual respect and appreciation!

This diorama is a team project of the 'German Gamblers': Christian Bruer, Frank Spahr, Guido Hopp and Torben Keitel; it was realised between May 2007 and November 2008.

Christian Bruer and Frank Spahr (translation)
November 2008

VMF-06 German Gamblers

Our very special thanks go to the Liverpool Old Mersey Times Public Relations Department for their kind support in any research for photos and information around the Liverpool Docks. A special thank-you goes also to Andreas Krause for his precise work with his milling machine on the polystyrene dock sections and Stefan Schacht for procuring the polystyrene sheet!

Here is a collection of photos of the Liverpool Docks Diorama. You will have already seen an overall view at the beginning of this section. You can get a good idea of the basic layout. Despite containing a large number of components, it does not appear crowded, and the builders have not been afraid to have empty areas. (Photos by the 'German Gamblers')

Here the basic arrangement of ships in the docks is being worked out at a preliminary stage. This is not the final disposition, as you can see by comparison with the previous photo, and in fact, there are a couple more merchant ships than made it into the final thing. But the point of this photo is to demonstrate the division of labour that a co-operative project allows. The ship makers have decided what they are building, and some ships have even been finished. The people concentrating on the docks are still in their planning stage, but the momentum of the whole project is not held up

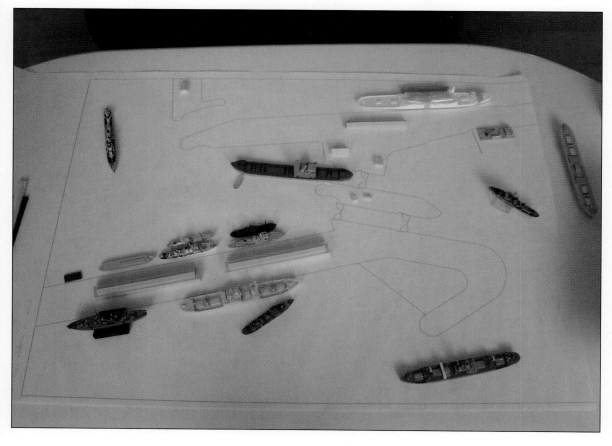

▼ This is one of the corvettes in a nearly completed stage. From the pennant number, ending in '8', I suspect it is HMS *Campanula*, though I am happy to be corrected. It looks to be based on a White Ensign kit.

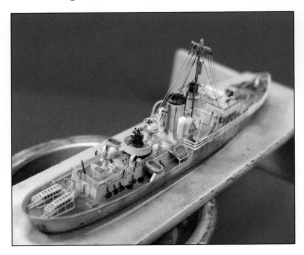

▶ This is one of the trawlers. Numerous fishing boats such as these were commandeered during both World Wars for escort work and minesweeping. They were also built specifically for Admiralty use. I don't know which one this is, or which kit is being used. Quite a lot of extra work has gone on here. Hatch covers, deckhouse roofs and extensions have been replaced or added. Notice the railings round the bridge and gun platforms. They have been covered with a film of PVA glue to represent the canvas dodgers

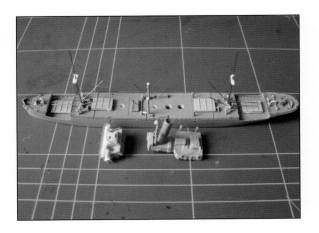

▲ This appears to be an ex-USGC cutter, supplied under Lend Lease. Presumably this is based on the White Ensign HMS *Gorleston* kit. The builder has evidently added extra parts from the spares box, such as the searchlight. Note how a strip of masking tape or similar has been used for the strake of plating on the hull. He also prefers to use his airbrush to start off doing the grime streaks on the hull

◀ One of the merchant ships. I don't know which one, or the source of the kit. It may be from Battlefleet, but I'm uncertain. The modeller here also likes to put lots of small details on prior to painting. I prefer to put my railings on last, after everything else is painted, on the grounds that otherwise I would be unable to get my brush in! Each to his own. I'm intrigued by the threaded and countersunk holes in the hull. They may be for holding the hull to the building board during construction. Or are they for screwing the ship to the base when it is completed, with the superstructure fitted as the final stage?

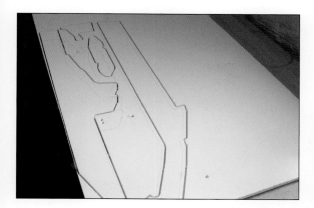

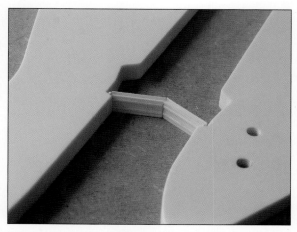

◀ A sheet of 6mm polystyrene sheet has gone through the milling machine. A lot of work has been saved here. If I had been invited to cut it all out by hand, I reckon I'd have claimed to be far too busy building ships!

▶ Lock gates made from polystyrene. With the River Mersey having a large tidal range, the docks would have dried out at low spring tide without these gates being able to close. Admittedly, ships are only able to enter the harbour at high tide during the springs, but you can't change nature, and at least it isn't the Bay of Fundy, in Canada!

▲ Here are the guys at one of their regular meetings. The arrangement here is different from that on the paper plan in the second photo, but has not reached the final arrangement. The darker grey merchant ship will take the place of the light one moored at the front quay, which will itself take the place of the one at the back, bound with masking tape, which will eventually be lost. Personally, I prefer this arrangement, because the foreground, as viewed from this direction, looks just a trifle empty in the completed diorama

◀ The docks have been fixed to the sea and preliminary painting of the water carried out. Most of the arrangement has been finalised, as paper cut-outs of the ships had been placed in position and sprayed over, and then their names marked. But there is still work to do with the big jetty, and small boats will be scattered here and there

▶ A complex framework is being built up here for the jetty. It looks as though the photo-etch has been custom made. That would be quite an expensive exercise. Alternatively, it might have been sourced from stuff that was intended for use in model railways, such as fancy fencing in OO scale. Whatever, it makes for an impressive and convincing structure

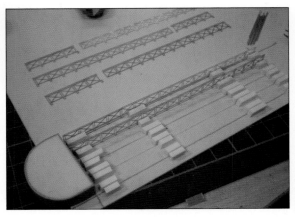

◀ The jetty is completed. The wooden pilings around the end seem to have been done by using heavily grooved plasticard which has been bent around a former. There now follows a selection of photos of the completed diorama, so that you can get a flavour of what an impressive and successful piece of work it is

MARE ISLAND NAVY YARD, BY BRUNO GIRE AND JEAN MAHIEUX

This is a joint project by two French modellers. It has been several years in the planning and making, and when it was displayed at Telford in 2011, it was still not finished. The plan was to make most of the models from custom designed photo-etch. Little tasters appeared on the Internet from time to time. It was obvious that this was a project that was far beyond the skills and aspirations of most ordinary modellers.

I am pleased to be able to present a few photos here, both of the whole composition, and of the construction process. I am not going to try to describe precisely how it has all been made. This is partly because I do not know, but also because I sincerely think that it deserves for Bruno and Jean to write their own book or series of articles!

▼ An overall view of the diorama, giving an impression of its scale, but not of the complexity involved. From left to right you can see accommodation barges, a merchant ship, a boom vessel, an enormous crane barge, a cruiser with an oil barge, a floating dry dock with a submarine, a slipway with submarines under construction and being launched, and finally the stern-wheel paddle ferry *Delta King*. (Photos by Jean Mahieux and Bruno Gire)

▲ The floating dry dock holding a submarine. Believe it or not, that is all made from photo-etch. They are not resin or plastic kits. You can see pieces of white plastic or card, peering out from underneath the hulls of the dry dock and also the workshop barge behind it. This indicates that the diorama was still under construction when these photos were taken

▲ The ferry *Delta King* bringing workers into the yards for their shifts

▶ The *Delta King* under construction. When you consider that this photo-etch was drawn and produced to make only one or two copies, and then multiply it many times over for all the other components, this must have been an incredibly expensive diorama to build, and an exercise in finding out just what it was possible to do

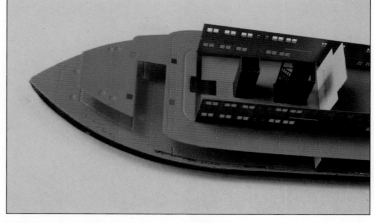

▼ Some of the various barges that were used in the yard

▲ I'm going to ask you once more to remember that these cranes were not built from commercially-produced kits but custom etched. It looks as though the complexity is well up there with the things that are coming out of the mainstream companies. It would be great if Bruno and Jean were able to make these available to the modelling public

DE REEDE VAN TEXEL

If you get the opportunity to visit the Netherlands, I strongly suggest you try and take a day to go across to the island of Texel. This is the most southerly of the West Frisian Islands. You can take your car or, more ideally, your bicycle on the ferry from Den Helder, which is about 45 miles north of Amsterdam. It is a pretty island, which you can cycle round in a day. It is open and windy, with a number of small villages and ecologically important sand-dunes.

Sheltered from the storms of the North Sea, the stretch of water between the island and the mainland, known as Texel Roads, was an important anchorage for Dutch shipping in the days of sail.

But if you are reading this book, your main reason for visiting Texel will be to go to the village of Oudeschild, and to visit the Kaap Skil maritime museum. Here is displayed one of the most amazing dioramas that you will ever see.

The Texel Roads diorama represents this area in the 1660s, at the height of Dutch naval power, and during the Anglo-Dutch wars. It is the result of

thirty five man-years of work. I can't remember whether that was five people working for seven years or seven people working for five, but it was thirty five in total. It is displayed in the basement of the new museum, which must have been designed and built to accommodate it and provide a suitable environment.

The diorama measures about 15 metres in length. It has somewhere in excess of 20 major vessels, three-masted and ship-rigged, with a much larger number of smaller craft, rowing boats, *jachts*, sloops, fishing boats, small trading craft, etc. Of the larger ships, there are Dutch naval vessels, Dutch East India Company ships, other merchant ships, and even a whaler. The village of Oudeschild is shown as it is thought that it looked like around that time, along with the fortifications that helped defend the anchorage from those nasty English!

The scale was chosen to correspond with one of the popular model railway scales, and enable commercially available parts, particularly figures, to be used.

It is my understanding that it does not depict the ships that were present on one particular day,

and that with a few exceptions, the models are representative of the various types of ships that would be seen here at that time. Almost all the ships are Dutch, although there is a British man of war that had been captured in battle.

Research for the ships began with consulting works of art, maritime scenes being a speciality of Dutch artists, and comparing these with ships' draughts that are surviving in the archives. From these, plans could be drawn up for a variety of types of ships and boats, and the decorative carvings designed. The idea was to make a number of master models from which resin copies could be made.

From the lines plan a basic hull shape, with no detail, was carved in wood, in two matching halves. These were placed in a vacuum moulding machine and a hollow polystyrene shell made of the hull. Standard plastic modelling techniques were used to detail the hull using plastic card and strip. Generic pieces of decorative carving had been made prior to this, and multiple copies cast in resin. The decoration on the bows and stern could then be built up with the minimum of effort.

When the hull, complete with decks, hatches and all the carved gingerbread work was finished, a silicone rubber mould was made, using an industrial-sized machine, and vacuum extraction of the bubbles. From this, resin copies were made,

▲ This is a general view of a bit more than half of the diorama. It extends to the left by about half as much again. The lighting levels vary in the display during a ten minute cycle, to try and imitate the passage of day and night, sunlight and storm. Interesting for the display, but it plays havoc with photography. The big pair of binoculars does not let you focus in on the diorama, but actually plays little CGI animations, depending on where you are looking with them

giving the ability to have identical or very similar ships of the same type or class.

The wood of the hulls was painted with brown paint and darker washes, and the brushes used for this part were varnish brushes of the size that furniture makers would use. Smaller details needed brushes of the sort of size we would normally use ourselves.

Masts and yards were probably made from wood, although I admit that I failed to ask this. Rigging is mostly various gauges of sewing thread and similar. It certainly looks as though original practice was followed for an authentic appearance. They did cheat a bit in some areas. For the shrouds and ratlines they had special photo-etched items made. But the deadeyes were made with proper holes that were laced in original fashion.

Most of the larger vessels have sails, either set or furled. It would appear that these were made from fine cotton fabric, stained with tea to take the stark whiteness out of it.

I am a little uncertain about how the figures were made. From my discussions with the guide at the museum, I understood that commercially available model railway figures were used. But from watching a short DVD about the construction of the model, the figures are elaborately dressed in seventeenth century fashion. Bearing in mind the thousands of figures needed for the whole thing, I imagine that a relatively small number of original figures were converted, and then multiple resin copies cast. That is what I would have done.

The earliest existing plans for the layout of Oudeschild date from the middle of the eighteenth century, nearly a century after the date that the diorama represents. The village must be regarded as somewhat conjectural. However, extensive research was carried out on the buildings that stand today in the village, to identify structures and building methods that could date from the seventeenth century, and would be valid for inclusion in the diorama.

Remains of an earthen fort still exist to the south west of the village, but appear to be only part of it. I suspect that the shoreline has shifted in the intervening centuries and half the fort has been washed away. The current remains seem much closer to the water's edge than the diorama indicates.

The diorama has been on display since completion in the year 2000. The current building seems to have opened only in the last few years, and the basement specially built to accommodate the diorama. The lighting is subdued and makes good photography difficult. Using a tripod, and keeping a small lens aperture to maximise depth of field, I was forced to expose each photo for about 30 seconds, which accounts for the ghostly figures walking in the background of some of them. The photos are perhaps not as good as I might have liked, but I think they give a flavour of what this model is all about, and the skill that has gone into it.

But, anyway, here are the photos that I took. And thanks to my wife for allowing us to take a detour on our holiday. After all, I did let her have a detour to her favourite patchwork quilting shop in Zutphen!

▼ These ships fly a flag with six bands of red, white and blue. This doubled-up Dutch flag was the naval ensign of the time

▲ This magnificent two decker would have been just about the largest ship in the Dutch fleet at this time. The English would have built a few that were larger, but the Dutch preferred ships that were rather more handy and with a shallower draught, in order to cope with their coastal waters. They also tended to be broader than the English ships, and therefore steadier and better gun platforms

◄ A close up of the same ship. You can appreciate the great breadth of this ship. It is a pity that I failed to get all of the stern into the photo, because you can just see how intricate the carving is

◀ These are three somewhat smaller vessels. They may all be merchant ships, but the one on the left could be a small warship. Notice the stern on the one at the right. It curves tightly in to a very small transom. This particular form was known as a 'flute'.

▲ A close up of one of the ships in the previous photo. Look at the level of detail incorporated into the hull. The regularity of the ratlines and the rather flat appearance of the deadeyes betray the fact that photo-etch has been used here. The officer on the poop deck with the red feather in his hat appears to be either looking through a large telescope, blowing a trumpet, or drinking a very big bottle of beer. Answers on a postcard, please

▶ This ship is in the process of being rigged. The mainmast shrouds have not yet been set up. When they have, the main topmast, which can be seen hanging in front of the lower mast, will be sent aloft. In addition, the fo'c'sle deck has not been built

◀ The diorama has a large number of small boats like this. I don't know if these would be known as 'sloops' or 'jachts' at this time. The one in front may be called a 'ketch jacht', due to the presence of a mizzenmast. Notice the 'leeboards' on the hulls. These are typical of Dutch craft, and also British spritsail barges. They can be lowered to act like a keel and prevent the vessel making too much leeway, and raised to negotiate shallow water

▶ This is a very workaday sort of ship. I think this one was described to me as being a whaling ship. If so, the Dutch must have had different techniques to those used in the nineteenth century, because I don't see much evidence of whaleboats, or davits to carry them

▲ Here is another two decker ship of the line, a bit smaller than the one in the earlier photo. Notice the way the lower gun deck steps down towards the stern. This might lower the centre of gravity and improve stability, but the leeward guns would be unworkable in any heavy sea. The decoration on the stern panel is a painting, rather than carving. Sailing out of the left side of the photo is a state *jacht*, presumably carrying the admiral to his flagship

◀ This ship has been beached, and is being pulled off by the boats with a rising tide. Perhaps it has been having the weed cleaned off its hull. The flag is that of the Dutch East India Company, so this is a high status merchant ship

CHAPTER 11

'THE SILVER DARLINGS'

*'We left our home grounds in the month of June,
And for canny Shields we soon were bearing,
With a hundred cran of the silver darlings,
That we'd taken from the shoals of herring'.*
Ewan McColl

In this chapter I am going to try and put everything together by demonstrating a large and complicated diorama that is almost totally scratch-built. It will involve boats, buildings, groundwork, figures and even horses. It is going against everything that I have said previously regarding my favourite scale being 1/700, as it is in 1/350 scale!

The theme is that of the Scottish herring fishing industry, in its heyday, at the end of the nineteenth century, just before the advent of steam power. Thousands of boats from towns and villages all along the east coast were involved, and the larger ones followed the migration of the shoals of fish during the year, starting in the Shetland Islands in the spring, moving down the coast during the summer, and culminating in the great autumn fishery, centred on Great Yarmouth in Norfolk.

Gangs of young Scottish women, the 'fisher lassies', followed the fleet of boats to work at gutting and packing the fish into barrels of brine, for export to Europe. Experienced workers would be able to gut anything up to 60 herrings in a minute, using a razor sharp knife. They would wrap their fingers in strips of cloth, or 'clooties', to improve grip and to protect against cuts and the effect of salt. This was a very hard life for the girls, having to spend six months away from home, and to modern eyes, being paid a pittance and commercially exploited. But the women later looked back and regarded it as the best time of their lives, with a sense of independence denied to most working class women in society.

For the men, the fishing industry was, and still is, fraught with danger, from injury and drowning, and the unpredictable weather of the North Sea.

The diorama depicts the harbour of Pittenweem, in Fife, in the year 1895, or thereabouts. I chose this village for several reasons. It has changed relatively little in the past hundred years. One of the piers was demolished and moved in 1905, to enlarge the inner harbour, but most of the buildings are the same. The size of the harbour was ideal for me to show a sizeable portion of it in 1/350 scale, and still be a manageable model of about 60cm x 40cm. I could pack the harbour with boats, so that it was possible to walk from one side to the other across the decks. It is documented that gutting and packing took place at Pittenweem, and that it was used as a base by visiting boats during the migration south.

The diorama shows the harbour in the morning. The boats have mostly returned from fishing, which took place overnight, racing back to the harbour, in order to get the fish unloaded in as short a time as possible. Scottish herring was always gutted and packed on shore, and had to be in the barrels within 24 hours of being caught, in order to receive the prized 'Crown Brand', and the best price.

The fish are put into the 'farlans', wooden troughs on the quayside, where the fisher lassies are gutting and then packing into the barrels, which are then loaded onto carts for transport to the railway station, half a mile away, up the hill.

The appearance of Pittenweem, as well as the lives of the workers, and the various types of boats used, are well documented. There are books consisting of old photographs produced by Stenlake Publishing, with names such as *Old Pittenweem*, *Old Crail* and *Old St Monans*. *Sailing Drifters* by Edgar J March and *Plank on Frame Models*, Vol 1 by Harold A Underhill give plans of typical Fifies and Zulus, the main types of boats used. On the Internet I found an Ordnance Survey map of Pittenweem, in 1/2500 scale, dated 1895, which gave me the exact shape of the harbour and the layout of the houses along the street. This meant I did not need to do a detailed topographical survey of the harbour, or extrapolate from the images of Google Earth, or a modern Ordnance Survey map.

The Scottish Fisheries Museum, a few miles along the coast at Anstruther, has a number of old models of fishing boats, as well as some real ones,

This is the harbour as it currently is. Most of the buildings have changed relatively little, although the one on the extreme left was built to replace one that was demolished around 1900, just after the date of the diorama. The pier from which this photo was taken was built around 1904. The previous pier was much closer to the opposite harbour wall, and the inner harbour must have been very cramped. I believe that the area of smooth stonework is the place where the old pier joined the main quay

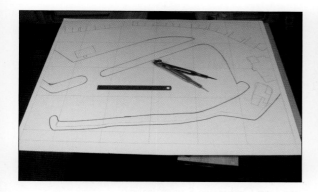

▲ The old Ordnance Survey gave me the shape of the harbour and the arrangement and sizes of the buildings. For reasons of copyright, I have not reproduced the map here, but this is a copy that I drew, enlarged to the scale of 1/350, to use as a template. Proportional dividers, such as these, are expensive but a very worthwhile investment for scratch-building, enabling you to avoid lots of tedious measuring and mathematical calculations

▲ This is going to be the base. There is a sheet of 6mm MDF, 60cm x 45cm. On top of this is glued a sheet of watercolour paper, which will represent the water surface. So much happened to this paper in the course of construction that it really did not serve any useful purpose. The quayside and piers are made from more 6mm MDF. The outer pier, at the bottom, in real life has a very distinct kink, very obvious from photos and Google Earth. I needed to make some adjustments to the shape later on.

including the Fifie *Reaper*, which has been superbly restored and is still afloat. These are particularly useful for details of the paint schemes that the boats carried. If you are in this part of Scotland, the East Neuk of Fife, then this museum is well worth spending a couple of hours in, as is also the fish and chip shop a few doors up the street!

I did a bit of my own research, by taking a couple of trips to the village to take lots of photographs of the buildings, the stonework of the old pier, and the rocks on the shore. I cannot be sure that buildings were painted the same colours in 1895 that they are now. Almost certainly they were

much more subdued and weather-beaten, but at least I can be fairly certain that a house that is plain stone in 2012, without plaster or paint, was the same in 1895.

The whole diorama took about a year to make. It was entered into the competition at the IPMS UK exhibition at Telford in 2012. It won a silver medal. I was disappointed in this as I thought it warranted gold, but I discovered that it had been marked down for a couple of mistakes of which I was aware. As well as rectifying these, the final few finishing touches have since been added.

So, come on, my Silver Darlings, let's get building!

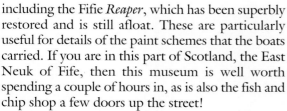

▶ Here is that kink. There was chisel work on one side of the pier and building out on the other. The raised sea wall was made with some strips of corrugated cardboard. The whole thing was then covered with a layer of Polyfilla. I have sanded it down to a vaguely smooth surface, and here you can see me giving the pier a rough texture with the Dremel-type tool. The real pier is extremely uneven stonework, and not the sort of place to wear stilettos or use a wheelchair. Other parts of the base will receive different treatments, depending on what the original surface might have been

▶ This was my first attempt at making the rocks outside the harbour wall. Even though I was going to texture the stone chippings with Polyfilla, you can see why I said, 'No, that ain't gonna do!'

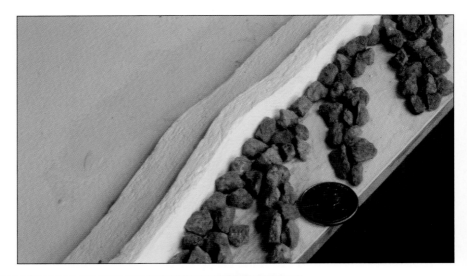

◀ This is much more like it! I simply built up some ridges of Polyfilla. When it was set, I went over it several times with different Dremel cutters to give the appearance of fingers of rock, with deep fissures and cracks, but still largely being solid. The cutter in the chuck is very thin and sharp. I think it is of dental origin, and good for deep cuts

▶ And this is what it all looks like after a few layers of paint have been applied. The stone on this part of the coast is sandstone of a rather bright ochre hue. Over a first coat of acrylic paint, I built up the colour with artist's oils; ochres, sandy browns and umbers; and washes of burnt umber, sepia and blacks

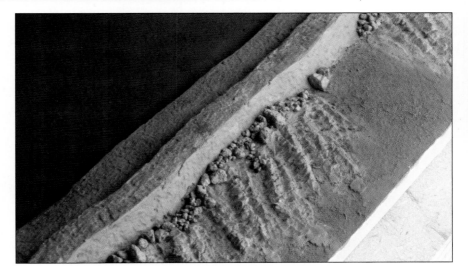

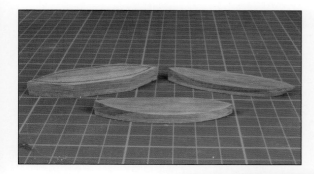

◀ Now we move onto the boats. These are the basic hull shapes. I used some walnut sheet that I found in my cupboard. It is not the ideal wood to use, as it is very hard and produces some very irritating dust. I shaped the hulls using a belt sander. I won't show you how, as I'm probably lucky to still have all my fingers. 'Don't try this at home.' The hull at the right shows the raking stern of the Zulu, while that in front has the straight stern of the Fifie. I made a total of ten hulls, of various sizes

▶ For the deck I used grooved plasticard, and plastic strip of appropriate size for the rubbing strakes, stem and stern posts, and for the bulwarks, which are surprisingly low. They are just high enough to trip up a sailor, but not high enough to stop him falling in the drink. They have a very distinctive appearance with exposed timberheads. Combined with a rail on the inboard side, this gives the appearance of a row of slots, and this is what I am trying to imitate with this Dremel cutter. When painted and given a dark wash, it will look OK

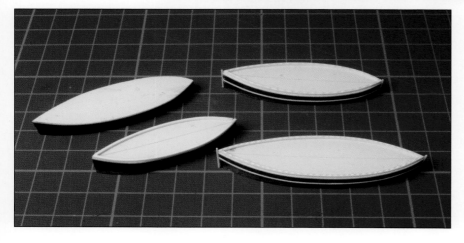

◀ This shows some of the masters at various stages of construction. You will notice that I have put no deck fittings or hatch coamings on them. This is because I wanted to be able to have every boat slightly different. Even though it would make more work for me in the long run, I did not want to cast absolutely identical boats

◀ These are the masters in a cardboard 'box', waiting for me to pour silicone rubber to make a mould. The mixing ratio for the catalyst in the stuff that I have got is so complicated that I need a calculator. I generally paint some of the mix over the masters first, try to avoid air bubbles, and then pour the rest. The mixture takes twenty-four hours to set, and any bubbles that have got incorporated during mixing rise to the surface and burst

▶ Everything is set up for casting. There is the mould, cans of resin and hardener (don't get the lids mixed up), mould release spray, disposable glasses for mixing, measuring cups, mixing sticks and an incredibly useful little brush

◀ As I am a doctor, I purloined a few of these brushes from work. They are used for taking cervical smears. They are great for brushing the resin into all the corners and completely fill the mould without voids. When the resin is fully solid, you can crack it off the bristles and use the brush again. Work very quickly, because the resin begins to go off and cure within a minute or two. You can slow the reaction down a bit by cooling the cans of resin and hardener in the refrigerator before mixing

▲ These are a couple of the castings that I made. Each of them contains one of each size of boat. I cast more than I knew I would need. This gave me a chance to sort out the best formed hulls and discard those with major casting flaws or big air bubbles. I am hardly an expert caster and am not capable of achieving a professional standard. I was willing to accept hulls with defects in the sides, because they would not be noticeable when packed together in the harbour

▼ Here are some hulls showing the various stages of completion of the deck details. At the left is a basic hull with nothing done to it. Next is one with the centre line marked, hole for the foremast drilled, and shape of fish hold and cabin roof drawn in. Then four with a variety of deck arrangements. You can see that I have put thwarts going across the boat, the housing into which the foremast will go when lowered, hold coamings, and cabin roofs in some. Finally two with the hold opened up by grinding with the Dremel and cleaning up with a file

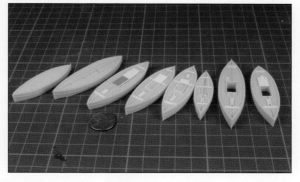

▲ The whole fleet ready for painting. I think they are all slightly different. The masts are brass rod of suitable diameters for the size of boat. In real life they were surprisingly thick, and were unsupported, apart from the burton and the halyard, which were running rather than standing rigging. It is not obvious in this photo, but the foremasts are raked slightly aft, and the mizzens have distinctly odd-looking forward rake

▲ These boats have been painted in the typical colour scheme of black hull with a white waterline that rises towards the bow. Perhaps that was a nineteenth century version of a 'go faster' stripe. I chose a variety of colours for the decks: plain wood, grey, brown and red lead. The models and boats in the Fisheries Museum show this, as well as the fact that blue was the predominant colour for the deck fittings. The yards are simply pieces of plastic rod, while the sails are made from cigarette paper. I only used a small rectangular or trapezoidal piece, rather than the full size sail. After gluing to the yard, the paper was painted with diluted PVA glue. This softened the paper, and enabled me to get it to fold and hang like canvas fabric

▲ I found making the buildings almost as interesting as the boats. You can see that I am using the proportional dividers to prick off distances on the photo and convert them to the correct size for the model. Basically I set the wider points to the width of the building on the photo, and the narrower to the size of the building's footprint on the base. It is also obvious how the converging verticals on the photo complicate matters. And the foreshortening of the verticals as the camera was pointing upwards means that the heights cannot be totally accurate. But I reckon that it's close enough

▶ The pieces of plasticard were glued to blocks of balsa wood, carved to shape. Roofs were made from grooved plasticard, or in some cases, scribed watercolour paper, if I wanted to replicate terracotta pantiles. This latter method did not work well on larger buildings and I ended up just using a layer of acrylic gel and impressing it with a vertical linear pattern

◀ It is necessary to check things frequently as you go along. As I worked from left to right, I found that I had a tendency to make things just slightly bigger, and had to constantly correct myself

▶ Here we have barrels cut from plastic rod and glued into piles. I did not attempt to try and get the true shape of a barrel. It would have driven me mad to do that for somewhere in excess of 700 of them! Baskets are cut from plastic tube, and the troughs, or 'farlans' are made from plastic strip. I'm rather pleased with the lampposts. I was just going to slip a piece of brass wire inside a bit of hypodermic needle. But when I trimmed off the green plastic, I found that the hard white plastic inside would do very well for the base of the pillar

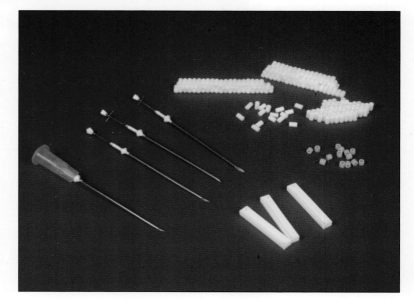

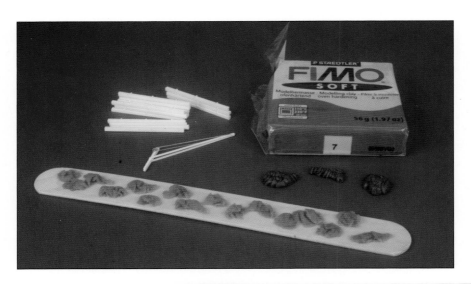

◀ Nets are made from bits of my wife's nylon tights, held in shape on a strip of double-sided tape, and then hardened with CA glue. Sacks of salt for preserving the herring are made from Fimo paste, which is hardened in the oven. The piles of plastic strip represent baulks of timber which were slotted into position across the entrance to the inner harbour to protect against winter storms

▶ The large spherical buoys are simply mustard seeds. I hope they don't start germinating! And held in position on the back of a pile of 'Post-it' notes you can see the various stages in making wheelbarrows, with pieces of copper wire for the handles. Although it is not very visible in the photo, the legs at the back end are just little dabs of acrylic gel

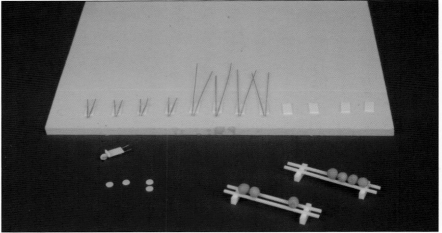

◀ Here I'm really having fun. I was racking my brains trying to work out how to scratch-build cartwheels in this scale. But then I discovered this sheet of hand-wheels, in laser-cut card by HMV of Hamburg. So here there are three carts, a milk float, four horses, one of those new-fangled horseless carriage contraptions, (they'll never catch on!) and even a baby's pram

▲ I'll now move on to show you the completed diorama. But first is an illustration of a mistake. I had painted and textured the water first, and then glued the boats to it. I ended up with gaps under the hulls, as you can see by the slips of paper. The diorama was marked down because of this fault at Telford in 2012. I was disappointed at first, but I can see that it was justifiable

▼ The boats are crowding into the harbour any way they can. The skippers were reputed to be very skilled at getting their boats into any gap that was available. In the period between the last photo and this one being taken, I have filled those gaps using Vallejo Still Water, which has the other advantage of smoothing out some of the sharpness of the ripples. It now looks much better

◄ These sails which are still hoisted were made from stuff slightly thicker than cigarette paper. The blocks and tackle on the rigging of all these boats was photo-etch, from Alliance Model Works

► Unloading the herring onto the pier. The fish are represented by sawdust, painted silver

▼ As far as I am aware, the large yellow house at the far end is now converted into apartments for holiday rentals. I have no financial interest in it

▲ The plastic of the buildings was roughened slightly with some of the acrylic paste that I use for waves. They were then painted with acrylics and details, depth and texture given with artist's oil paints. At the right you can see the blue and yellow milk float, and women buying milk by the jug-full

◀ The fisher lassies at work. There are about 300 figures in the diorama, in resin, by L'Arsenal. Sixty or so had to undergo 'gender reassignment surgery'. This mainly involved building up skirts using acrylic gel, and sanding down the hat to look more like a headscarf

▲ When I had glued all the boats onto the base I realised that the way they were orientated drew the eye automatically to this point on the quayside. It needed a point of focus. So this is a fish auction. Samples of fish from boats that are not already contracted to a particular packer are being examined and bid for

It has taken me about three years to build all the dioramas for this book. Now that I've finished, I'm rather looking forward to making one or two single ships. I wonder if I'll have forgotten how to do it?

I know, I'll go and buy a copy of my first book!

SUPPLIERS AND DEALERS

Here are some website addresses and telephone numbers of suppliers and dealers that I have found useful. I hope you do too.

White Ensign Models
The major UK online supplier of ship kits and accessories.
www.whiteensignmodels.com
+44 (0)1568 709149   UK
+1 304-872-4212   USA

Dorking Models
A wide range of models, including HP Models.
www.dorkingmodels.co.uk
+44 (0)1306 881747   UK

L'Arsenal
French resin producer and supplier of kits.
www.larsenal.com

Free Time Hobbies
Major American online hobby store.
www.freetimehobbies.com
+1 706-946-1120   USA

Jamieson's Models
My favourite local hobby shop
30 Saltmarket
Glasgow
Scotland
+44 (0)141 552 3956   UK

Battlefleet Models
For all those harbour craft and freighters.
www.battlefleetmodels.com
+1 720-369-6508   USA

Hamburger Modellbaubogen Verlag
Excellent German paper model producers.
www.papermodel.com

Acrylic sheet (Perspex) can be got in the UK from
www.sheetplastics.co.uk
+44 (0)1455 698466   UK

I am always going on about 'Caenis' fly-tying thread for rigging. You can get it in the UK from:
Glasgow Angling Centre
www.fishingmegastore.com
+44 (0)871 716 1670   UK

or in the USA from:
J Stockard
www.jsflyfishing.com
+1 860-927-1100   USA